ORGANIC NETWORKER®

DISCOVER THE 12 ORGANIC PRINCIPLES FOR LIMITLESS WEALTH

KOSTA GARA

BLOOMBERG

PUBLISHING™

U.S.   Canada   Mexico   Hong Kong   Australia

Published by Bloomberg Publishing, Inc., Dover, Delaware

Interior Design by Rachael Urrutia

ISBN 978-0-9837669-0-2

Printed in the United States of America

PREFACE

I believe everything happens for a reason.

Network marketing has allowed me to build a lifestyle that has exceeded my wildest dreams. I became a millionaire by age thirty-one and have travelled the world. I co-authored the Amazon bestseller, *Guerrilla MLM Marketing*, and was featured in *Forbes* and *Inc. Magazines*, *Televisa* and *Cronica*. Most importantly, I mentored 36 individuals from multiple countries around the world who became millionaires in network marketing. As a result, I was fortunate to retire at the age of 33 for eighteen months and again at 37 as a multimillionaire. I am blessed and privileged to live in a country that cherishes freedom.

The heart and soul of this book are my *12 Organic Principles for Success*, which have become the foundation for my personal and financial achievements. I did not pull these 12 principles out of thin air. I did not learn them in an MBA program, nor did I come up with them while building my network marketing business.

They came from a journey where I was forced, as a young boy, to make decisions that would someday define the man I would become. I survived my youth by discovering what I was made of, and along the way, I also discovered what I stood for. I learned that all of the goodness life has to offer is available to you when you are willing to combine consistent effort with a set of self-defining principles.

My journey began in 1979, when I was seven years old. The Iranian Revolution erupted, changing the course of my life forever. Fanatical Iranian revolutionists took brutal control of the country. Anyone who disagreed with them or had any allegiance to the Shah were indiscriminately subject to hangings or beatings. I vividly recall the terror that consumed me, seeing men beg for their lives as a makeshift hangman's noose was placed around their necks. I can still hear the crowds cheering as a construction crane lifted them twenty feet into the air. I felt sick, as I watched their writhing bodies struggle and die.

Public beatings were a daily occurrence. Etched deep into my memory are the agonizing screams of a young teenage boy, who made the intolerant mistake of holding hands with his girlfriend in public, stripped to his waist, mercilessly beaten with a heavy leather belt tearing the skin from his body.

My father, my hero, was arrested for nothing more than being a high-ranking military officer in charge of Embassy security. After a twenty-minute trial by a cleric, he was sentenced to three years in Evin prison, known as *Hell on Earth*, where he endured unimaginable mental and physical brutality. A broken man, he was released three years later, and shortly afterwards died of a massive heart attack.

The day my father was arrested, his monthly salary was terminated. With no income, my mother and I had to find a means to put food on the table and keep a roof over our heads.

We worked everything that came our way. I was learning very early in life what it takes to survive under extremely hazardous conditions.

An excellent seamstress, my mother began to build a seamstress business. I helped by blanketing our neighborhood with flyers, knocking on doors and telling them that Mom was the best seamstress in Tehran. Women had to cover their heads in public. Mom got a job at a factory that made scarves. I would go with her to the Grand Bazaar to buy rolls of cloth, and I observed the process of producing the scarves and preparing them for market. Mom was an excellent cook. On my eighth birthday, my family had a party for me at a local park. I saw that people were selling food in the park and told Mom that we should open a food booth. She reluctantly agreed to give it a try for one weekend. I designed a booth and made a sign, and Mom baked pastries. Even at the tender age of eight, I knew that the broader I smiled and the more convincing I was about Mom's terrific cooking, the more I would sell. What excited me most was the thought of how proud my father would be when he found out I was taking care of Mom, as I had promised. Fortunately, I had sold all of the pastries before violence broke out and a student was shot and killed, which ended my food booth business.

Through a friend who bribed officials, we had an agreement that they would supply us with high-fashion clothing, accessories, and cosmetics from Paris and London, and we would sell them in our home. Iranian women loved these luxuries, but when the revolution began, they were no longer allowed to wear them. They would come to our home wearing scarves covering their heads, chadors that covered their entire bodies, and no makeup. Immediately upon entering our home, they would shed their drab garb and tried on the high-fashion clothes and accessories and applied makeup, morphing into beautiful women. It was my first experience of seeing women look into a mirror and admiring themselves. I appointed myself store manager and cashier.

The business was highly illegal, but we had to make money. It lasted until the officials would no longer take bribes, as they would have been executed by hanging, if caught.

My life took another unexpected turn the day the fanatical citizen army, the Basij, came to my school wearing green and white headbands with the words, *To Die for the Glory of God*. They recruited young men and boys by enticing them with special privileges and instant access into heaven when they died. Millions of males were slaughtered by willingly running across Iraqi mine fields during the Iran-Iraq war. When I came home wearing a Basij headband, Mom knew she had to take drastic measures. Men and boys were not allowed to leave the country, so she pulled me out of middle school, sold everything she owned, and hired a smuggler to take me out of the country, knowing she may never see me again.

My smuggler and I travelled by bus to a treacherous northern mountain range, and then journeyed by foot and horseback for seven days. I suffered bleeding blisters on my feet and saddle sores that bled through my pant, freezing weather, hunger, and exhaustion, while evading military patrols and bounty hunters. I thought my misery had ended the night I crossed into Turkey to a safe house, hours from meeting my mother, who was waiting for me in Van, Turkey.

At three o'clock in the morning, I was wrenched from a deep sleep by Turkish police, who smashed down the door to the safe house. I was arrested for the high crime of trying to leave Iran to escape the tyranny of the radical Islamic regime and live free, and I was handed over to the Iranian authorities. On my thirteenth birthday, I was sitting in a maximum-security prison, having been tortured. Through the gripping pain and loneliness, I wondered if my mother or other family member would ever find me and if prison was where I would die.

Six months later, an uncle located me and arranged a bribe for my release. Although I was no longer incarcerated, Iran became my prison, as I was forbidden to leave the country. In attempt to avoid the revolutionary guard, who were constantly looking for young boys to fight in the Iran-Iraq war, I moved from relative to relative.

Tired of living in tyranny and having no place to call home, I asked my uncle to help me locate a smuggler to take me out of the country, knowing if I were caught trying to escape a second time the punishment would be unforgiving. The escape was successful, and I was reunited with my mother, who had been waiting for me for a year in Van, Turkey.

While I had escaped Iran, Turkey was laced with police and bounty hunters on the lookout for young men who had escaped Iran. Determined to live free, my mother and I made our way through Turkey and, with the help of a smuggler, crossed the Evros River into Greece. All we had in our possession were six sugar cubes. As the sugar cube was dissolving in my mouth, to me it was the sweet taste of freedom.

My autobiography, *Six Sugar Cubes*, is a story about my journey from tyranny to freedom.

ACKNOWLEDGMENTS

My life's journey has been a blessing in that I have met thousands of people along the way who have inspired and nurtured me. It is my honor to acknowledge these selfless individuals.

I owe my deepest debt of gratitude to my mother Minoo, a widow who single-handedly raised me through my formative years. Under the most difficult circumstances, she made a decision to put me in the hands of a smuggler and send me on a journey to freedom. Although there was a possibility she would never see me again, she chose to risk it all in order for me to grow and blossom under the umbrella of freedom. Her guidance prepared me for the success I have today.

I am deeply grateful to my father, who began teaching me CANEI (Constant And Never Ending Improvement) at a very young age. Unbeknownst to me, CANEI was becoming hardwired into my DNA.

Genuine thanks to my relatives for the love and support they gave to my mother, sister, and me during a time when we needed it the most.

Heartfelt gratitude to the humble villagers and tribesmen who risked their lives to house me during my journey as a young boy, from tyranny to freedom; the people of Turkey and Greece who were incredibly kind to my mother and me, the Canadian government for accepting my mother and me and for igniting the entrepreneurial fire that burned deep within me, and the United States of America for giving me the privilege to live and work in this beautiful country.

Sincere thanks to my best friend and one of the most influential individuals in my life Terry LaCore, businessman and CEO of multiple highly successful companies. Through him, I've come to realize how one person can touch your life in so many amazing ways. Terry has gone above and beyond the call of any human-itarian duty to support, guide, and advise me in my life as a mentor and friend. Thank you, Terry, for all you do and have done for me. You have enabled me to write this book and share my life experiences. You are truly an icon and a visionary the world is fortunate to have.

Deepest thanks to a mentor and dear friend Nicki Keohohou, the founder and CEO of DSWA (Direct Selling World Alliance), who badgered, encouraged, and motivated me until I committed my first thought to paper for this book. Nicki is one of the most sought-after and admirable women in the network marketing profession and one of the kindest human beings I have ever known.

My gratitude goes to Terry Pfitzer, whose insight and input helped me craft a first draft that became the organic blueprint that guided me throughout the writing of this book.

I am especially appreciative for writer Dr. Michael Gonzalez and his wife JennieLee for the painstaking task of rewriting and polishing the *Organic Networker* manuscript to book form.

Special thanks to the thousands of networkers from around the globe who have joined me in helping to improve the lives of thousands of people from all walks of life.

Also, a sincere thank you to my many close friends, colleagues, and mentors who encouraged me to put my hard-won life journey and professional wisdom into this book. It would take several pages to name all of you, but you know who you are.

Last but not least, my deepest gratitude goes to Katie Kezele, my assistant who spent countless hours for being the liaison between editors, proof-readers, the publishing company, designers, distribution channels and everybody else in between that was somehow involved in contributing to this book. I could not imagine completing this without her, and I am forever grateful for her presence in my life.

SECTION ONE
ABOUT ORGANIC NETWORKING

Chapter 1

MY 12 ORGANIC PRINCIPLES FOR SUCCESS

I developed an understanding of my *12 Organic Principles for Success* through trial and error. They were not handed to me on a silver platter. They have been honed throughout my life journey, and I am guided by them, personally and professionally, on a daily basis.

Organic Networker is the harmony and integration of ideas, concepts, and my *12 Organic Principles for Success*. You will discover that the subtleties of each organic principle will collectively contribute to the success you wish to achieve.

Principle #1—Readiness = Preparation + Organization

Have you ever heard of anyone preparing for failure? I have sponsored hundreds of potential leaders into my network marketing business that failed because they didn't prepare or weren't organized. There was nothing to be ready for. I am blown away by the many highly talented people I have sponsored, from all walks of life, who set up a first-class home office. Then, to my surprise, they might make a half-dozen calls, of which all six prospects decline their offer, and they quit. I soon realized that being prepared and organized without being ready or having a Plan B, if Plan A didn't work, was useless.

The Iranian revolution turned my family's world upside down. My mother learned that my elementary school teachers were teaching my classmates and me how to fire assault weapons. Young boys were being recruited by the Basij, the citizens' army, and sent to the front line of the Iran-Iraq war. When I came home wearing a Basij green and white headband with the words, *To Die for the Glory of God*, my mother pulled me out of school. She knew it would be a matter of days before the authorities would come looking for me. She was forced to make a snap decision to hire a smuggler to help me escape the country immediately. There was little time for preparation and organization, and we had to be ready the moment my smuggler called and gave the green light. We had a Plan A, with no Plan B, and I ended up in a maximum-security prison.

In network marketing, Plan B is a must. The type of leader I look for is someone who is willing to learn and implement preparation and organizational skills and understands that readiness means having a Plan A, as well as a Plan B. Let's say you have a meeting with a prospect at a coffee shop twenty minutes away. Just as your coffee is being served, your cell phone rings, and your prospect cancels the appointment. What do you do? Is your time wasted and you go home? Or, are you prepared and organized, ready to productively maximize your time? With your Plan B in place, you take advantage of the opportunity and make a few prospecting or follow-up calls, prepare for your upcoming event, or meet with another prospect in the area who is available to fill in the timeslot.

Remember, being prepared and organized doesn't mean everything will be flawless. When things don't go as planned, always have a Plan B ready. Take this principle to heart in business and in your personal life; it will help lower your stress level and move you one step closer to the lifestyle of your dreams.

Principle #2—Discipline = Focus + Dedication

Are you focused to succeed? I mean, do you have a burning desire to succeed in network marketing? Focus and dedication are the two most essential ingredients that you must incorporate to sustain the level of discipline necessary to achieve success in this industry.

It is important to focus on your vision in order to achieve your goals. Are you aiming at your target through a laser telescope to ensure that you hit it dead center, or are you using a shotgun, trusting you will be rewarded for hitting any part of the target? Focus and dedication is the litmus test as to whether your efforts will bear the fruit of success or failure.

In order to wrap your mind around the discipline needed to succeed, commit to paper the most important goal you wish to achieve. For the moment, let's assume that goal is to earn $10,000 per month. Remember, a goal is the end result. The activities you do to attain that goal are the organic building blocks to achieve your goal.

An activity you must master to earn $10,000 per month is to make 10 prospecting calls, warm or cold market, six days per week. Having the discipline to succeed is where the pretenders are separated from the contenders.

I have never been one to beat around the bush. If you are determined to become a successful organic networker and take control of your life, draw a line in the sand and have the courage to implement the discipline necessary to achieve your goals. I will guide you toward your goals, but it is not my responsibility to motivate you. If you have the discipline to make 10 prospecting calls per day, every day except on Sunday, the results you experience will be all the motivation you'll need to become an elite organic networker.

The day I left Tehran with my first smuggler, I was dedicated and focused, and I knew that I needed the discipline to endure the journey that would fulfill my goal, which was to live free from tyranny. The night that my mother and I crossed the Evros River into Greece, all we possessed were the clothes on our back and six sugar cubes that my mother had wrapped in her purse. As I think back to that moment, I enjoyed my sugar cube, not because it satisfied my hunger, but because it represented the sweet taste of freedom.

Many people have asked me how I was able to achieve the lifestyle I enjoy today. As I have often stated, if I were stripped of everything I own today, I'd regain it all because the experiences I dealt with from early childhood have ingrained the discipline I need to organically rebuild.

I did not succeed in my first network marketing attempt, but I did not fail. I experienced missteps but not missed steps. These initial missteps were my opportunity to learn and grow, which prepared me for my second attempt in network marketing, just as it did in my second effort with escaping tyranny. I committed to staying focused and dedicated to making 10 warm or cold market calls per day. It didn't matter if I was consumed with the fear of rejection, was ill, if I had someone hang up on me, or if my favorite soccer team was competing in the World Cup championship. I stayed focused and dedicated until this activity became hardwired into my brain. I learned from my many missteps in my first attempt at network marketing, but by implementing discipline into my second attempt, within 18 months I became the youngest millionaire in that company.

I competed in wrestling when I was in high school. A little older than my competitors, my goal was to be the best wrestler in my weight class. While my teammates were hanging out, doing what teenagers do, I would spend a couple of extra hours on school days and weekends mastering the fundamentals, improving my technique, and working through the grueling, getting-in-shape regimen to take me to the top of my game. By having the discipline and being focused and dedicated to my goal, I won several medals and earned a $40,000 university scholarship.

Escaping from a country where tyranny was the rule of law and ending up in Canada, a country where personal and business achievement was encouraged was a breath of fresh air. My good fortune was incomprehensible. I could work, attend school, compete in sports, and pursue my dreams of a better future. I was an immigrant who did not speak English. At times, I was overwhelmed, but I quickly embraced the challenges, drew a line in the sand, and defied anyone who tried to deny me the right to work and fulfill my dreams. I understood I needed to be focused and dedicated to my goals and have the discipline to achieve them.

I now enjoy living a lifestyle I had only dreamed of, but more importantly, I've mentored and helped thousands of people change their lives, and many became millionaires by embracing discipline.

Principle #3—Organization = Preparation + Diligence

On my first attempt to escape Iran, my mother and uncle's inability to pay attention to details was a very tough and almost unforgiving lesson for me, but in the long run, it has become one of my core strengths and has been a principle guide in formulating my *12 Organic Principles for Success*.

After the horrifying experience I had with my first smuggler, when seeking my second smuggler, my uncle took the time to get organized and do the preparation and diligence necessary for my escape to freedom. He found a reputable smuggler who laid out the exact plan for my escape, the route, the dangers posed by bounty hunters, the forces of nature, and the consequences if I were captured, all of which was in contrast to my first smuggler. We travelled by vehicle, instead of hiking and horseback riding.

Because we were organized, I was reunited with my mother within days and living in a free country.

My flight to freedom taught me that, when it comes to building a business, being organized is paramount, and by being prepared and being diligent and anticipating the challenges, the road to success becomes easier to follow.

When it comes to organization, we are all born with our unique DNA, and perhaps some of us inherit organization genes. Regardless of our genetic inheritance, we all have the ability to acquire some level of organizational skill. I was lucky, as I believe I inherited my father's organizational skills, which help me tremendously when I am multitasking. It is not necessary to go to extremes to keep yourself organized, but being prepared and then diligently following through will help make each task easier and more efficient, which will result in better time management.

Like success, being organized comes over time. Your desired result must be crystal clear before you can prepare for it.

Principle #4—Consistency = Commitment + Discipline

In order to succeed, whether it is with friendships, matters of the heart, or business, you need to have commitment and discipline and be consistent with your efforts.

I don't think you would be happy if your employer paid your weekly salary every four to five weeks, or your monthly salary every two to three months. Not only would you feel unappreciated, you would be enraged that their inconsistency would be responsible for your having missed a car or house payment.

In matters of the heart, couples fall passionately in love, every day, and can't wait to spend every waking moment together, cuddling and cooing. They are utterly absorbed with one another.

However, without commitment and discipline, the flame of their passion begins to diminish. Inconsistent passion is like a shooting star that streaks across the sky and flames out in the blink of an eye. True love is about the commitment and discipline needed to sustain passion and for love to blossom into a long-term, consistent relationship.

When I joined my second network marketing company, I knew the only way to achieve my goals was to commit to a plan of action and discipline myself to work it consistently, every day. I committed to making ten new prospecting calls per day, in addition to follow-up and three-way calls. I committed to attend weekly business briefings and to always bring someone new. Of course, there were times I wanted to give in to temptation, take a few days off, go to a movie, or attend a concert, but I told myself that if I achieved my goals, there would be ample time for entertainment. By being consistent in my efforts, eighteen months later I was a millionaire and was in total control of my life.

Having the commitment and discipline to do a job or task begins with you. What you might perceive as drudgery, such as making warm and cold prospecting calls, slowly transforms into fun, as you begin to experience results and can actually see your goals on the horizon. It is not unlike going to the gym for the first time, as it takes commitment and discipline and working on your goals, consistently, to get into shape. You attack the machines with a vengeance and wake up the next morning unable to move. You want to quit; it's too much work, but with commitment and discipline, results begin to happen. Now, you're having fun and can't wait to get to the gym. In network marketing, take a calendar and block out your commitment time frame. Then, map out your action plan, the activities you must commit to and be disciplined to do on a daily basis to reach your goal. What may seem scary or feel like drudgery, in the beginning, becomes fun as you experience results because of your consistent work ethic.

With commitment and discipline, as an organic networker you will not be a shooting star, quickly flaming out. Instead, you will be in control of your future, as I am, because you will have learned how to consistently work toward your goal.

Principle #5—Initiative = Passion + Action

Initiative and its synonyms—inventiveness, creativity, ingenuity, enterprise, resourcefulness, edge, and advantage—ooze with passion. When coupled with action, initiative can become an unstoppable force.

What makes the word, initiative, so intriguing is that it has no boundaries. It's a word that is uniquely yours and is only limited by the breadth of your imagination. Think about it. You get to decide what is possible. As an organic networker, I urge you to never harness your initiative. If your passion is powerful, it will propel you into action, and your initiative will become a proactive business-building machine in helping you achieve your goals. You will be willing to take calculated risks and plunge into activities that might have frightened you in the beginning of your career, such as cold-calling prospects who earn more money than you, are more educated than you, are in the medical profession, or people who you thought would never be interested in your opportunity. Do not let obstacles, like fear, intimidation, rejection, or no-shows test your initiative. Turn them into a learning tool.

Here is an example of the power of initiative. You invited dozens of people to your home for a business briefing over several weeks. Several people attended the briefings, and for all your effort, only one prospect joined. Think this scenario is depressing? What if that one person was destined to become a superstar and one of the top income earners in the industry? Take my advice: When one prospect attends a business briefing at your home and the ten others you invited are no-shows or not interested in your opportunity, look be-hind that one person sitting before you and imagine the thousands of people sitting behind him or her, who they will bring to your fledgling organization. If this thought doesn't flame your passion for action to take the initiative to grow your business, nothing will.

Initiative is about the urgency to do it, now.

Principle #6—Persistence = Vision + Willpower

Persistence is having a vision of where you are and where you want to go and having the willpower to fulfill your dreams. When it comes to defining your vision and the life you dream of, you have two choices: (1) accept your circumstances as they are, or (2) take ownership of your vision, empower yourself with the willpower to draw a line in the sand and move forward. If you are willing to embrace the second choice, the synergy of vision and willpower will equal the persistence required to meet your goal.

Persistence has become the foundation of who I am today. When I was seven years old, the Iranian revolution swept my beloved country and the new regime took power. The peaceful, ideal life I enjoyed was changed forever. At eleven years old, soon to be old enough to be drafted into the bloody Iran-Iraq war, my mother was faced with a very difficult decision. She could accept the life that the religious fanatics were forcing upon us or draw a line in the sand and dare anyone or anything to stop her from the dreams she had envisioned for my future. When my mother made the decision to hire a smuggler to help me escape the country, there was no turning back, and she understood that there could be severe and unforgiving consequences if I was caught trying to escape.

Having the willpower to pursue your vision until it becomes a reality takes persistence. To me, willpower is one of the most fascinating words in the English language. I am convinced that anyone can change personal circumstances, but not everyone has the willpower to do so. After I was released from prison, I was forced to return to Tehran. My circumstance hadn't changed;

I was in exactly the same place as before my first attempt to escape freedom. Once again, I was living in tyranny, moving from house to house so that the Basij would not find me and be forced into the military and sent to the front lines of the Iran-Iraq war. My circumstance was intolerable. I wanted to escape and be reunited with my mother, who was waiting for me in Van, Turkey.

The day I decided to leave, I told my uncle that if I had to walk to Turkey in the dead of winter, I would do it, and no one or nothing was going to stop me. I was not willing to accept living in tyranny. The willpower I could feel surging through my body, when I made the decision, gave me the courage to draw a line in the sand and persist at fulfilling my dreams of a better future.

Think of Willpower as the name of the most powerful stallion on Earth. Think of yourself as Persistence, sitting in the saddle. Persistence has sworn in a posse that is made up of some pretty tough guys, named: Doggedness, Tenacity, Determination, Resolve, Perseverance, and Resolution. The posse has one goal—to stay with you until you have achieved the willpower to pursue your vision.

When my mother and I lived in Greece, I worked in a fiberglass plant, cleaned foul-smelling ships, and waited tables at a restaurant. I was the breadwinner and had no time for school, but I was very content with my circumstances. I was living in a beautiful city, surrounded by friendly people, happily supporting my mother, had money in my pocket, hung out with friends, and played soccer and basketball every day. Living day to day was as good as it was going to get. I had no vision of my future beyond the next day, but that was okay with me.

However, I began to feel I wanted more out of life than what I had in Greece and made a decision to immigrate to a country that had more to offer. My mother and I applied and were accepted by the Canadian government. Within a few months we landed in Toronto, Canada, and an incident happened that I will never forget. As the taxi was taking us to the housing project where we would live, in my limited broken English I asked the driver what Canada was like. His response was, "It's the land of opportunity." This statement immediately triggered all the dreams I thought of when I was in solitary confinement. I suddenly realized that my mother and I could own a home and get good-paying jobs. It was at that moment that I decided I was going to enroll in school, look forward to making new friends, and play soccer and basketball. I was excited and, for the first time in many years, had a vision for my future and the willpower to fulfill my dreams. I knew it would take a great amount of persistence, but I knew I could do it. I felt it deep in my soul.

Once my mother and I settled into our home in Canada and I enrolled in school, it was time to put up or shut up. I had attended about six years of public school in Iran but had not attended school in Turkey or Greece. My vision of returning to school and improving my life seemed a little intimidating, given the fact that I was 18 years old and about to enroll as a freshman in high school. I spoke very limited English and had a heavier beard than most of my teachers. I enrolled in ESL (English as a Second Language) classes, studied diligently, and took my lumps as the new kid on the block. From where I had come, a little razzing didn't bother me. I always had a smile plastered on my face, and my gregarious nature began to win over friends. I was persistent and did something every day to improve myself and be accepted by my classmates. Then one day I made a major breakthrough. I discovered that basketball, a sport I had grown to love in Greece, was a universal language, and I could speak basketball very well.

After a year in Toronto, longtime friends of our family invited my mother and me to move to Ottawa, where they lived. They helped us secure a two-bedroom condo and helped me get a part-time job as a jeweler, which allowed me to support my mother. I was ecstatic. I was enrolled in high school, making very good progress academically, competing in sports, and had a job that paid $100 per week, of which I banked $30. I personified Persistence, riding my trusty stallion, Willpower. I was beginning to understand what the cabbie meant when he said that Canada was the land of opportunity. The vision of infinite opportunity danced in my head.

When my vision broadened, I left my part-time job as a jeweler and took a full-time job working the graveyard shift at a hotel. I was responsible for the night audit functions, checked in late arrivals, tackled my ESL lessons and other homework, caught a cat-nap, clocked out at 7:00 a.m., and three bus transfers later, I was home, where I grabbed a quick bite, took a shower, and bolted out the door in time to attend my first class. Friends would ask me how I did it. The answer that always ran through my mind was, how do I do what? All I could see was the light at the end of the tunnel, the vision of my future.

I compressed my love of sports into my hectic schedule and won numerous medals in wrestling and swimming. Upon graduation from high school, I was awarded a $40,000 university scholarship, payable at $10,000 yearly. I was thrilled beyond imagination. I had gone from being confined to solitary in a maximum-security prison in Iran to a university scholarship in Canada. I was extremely appreciative of my good fortune.

Persistence is:

* Getting knocked down and not blaming anyone and not making excuses.

* Drawing a line in the sand and daring anyone or anything to stop you.

* Jumping back on your stallion, Willpower, gathering your posse, and continuing your march toward your vision. If you don't have the willpower it takes, be honest with yourself and accept mediocrity.

❖ Welcoming hardship and setbacks and treating them simply as challenges you will overcome.

❖ Embracing hardships and setbacks.

During my second network marketing venture, I presented the business opportunity to 300 prospects. All but eleven said, no. I kept my eyes focused on my vision for financial security and lifestyle and never got off my stallion, Willpower. I became the poster child for persistence. Out of the eleven prospects that said, yes, six made a minimal effort. Five prospects, who imprinted their vision indelibly into their brain, jumped on their stallion, Willpower, and embraced persistence as though their lives depended on it. They went on to become millionaires.

Principle #7—Patience = Endurance + Vision

How many times have you heard a motivational speaker or highly successful leader say something like: Success in our profession isn't a sprint; it's a marathon, and when you hit the wall, envision your dreams that wait for you when you cross the finish line.

Although I understand the statement, I had no idea what the speaker was talking about. I had never run a marathon, much less trained for one. I simply knew the distance of a marathon was over 26 miles. As I began to look into the dynamics of running a marathon, I began to learn that it takes vision, endurance, and an enormous amount of patience. To compete in a marathon is one thing, but to compete at the elite professional level is another thing. I discovered that elite runners condition, physically and mentally, running hundreds of miles for months, enduring injuries and cramps that would give most athletes an excuse to quit, but they endure. They consume foods that will help them achieve their goal, not only to finish, but to win. And, they envision the finish line long before it's visible. This is vitally important, because on some level during the race, they will have to go to war with their body and mind that beg them to quit before the pain becomes excruciating and impossible to deal with.

I often compare running a marathon to my journey to freedom. Hiking long hours, withstanding the bitter cold weather, on horseback while enduring excruciating pain as the skin peeled away from my thighs, then hitting the wall by being arrested and sent to a maximum-security prison. It all became worthwhile when I was just a mile from the finish line and then finally reunited with my mother and living free of tyranny. My marathon journey was a personal endurance test. Eventually, the process made sense, especially being patient. When I arrived in Canada and started high school at the age of 18 and did not speak English, I was so far behind academically that, if my vision of graduating and being accepted at a university was to happen, I would need the patience to endure and overcome the obstacles in front of me.

In my network marketing career, I began to realize, if I was ever going to become an elite organic networker, I would need an enormous amount of patience. I would have to patiently spend hundreds of hours, month after month, sponsoring new prospects, retain them, and help them earn money. I knew that my mind would try to convince me to quit when I hit the wall, rejection. I knew that hitting the wall was one thing; enduring and crossing the finish line was another.

I didn't want to run my network marketing marathon alone. I wanted to build a team of elite marathon runners. That's when I came up with an idea handed to me by America's national pastime, baseball. Winning a marathon is an individual accomplishment; winning the baseball World Series is a team effort. What they have in common is that they both take vision, endurance, and a vast amount of patience.

As I thought about baseball's farm system, I began to realize it emulates our industry. From childhood, most players are filled with the dream of playing in the major leagues. Some quit after high school, while others go on to play college baseball. Some quit because of injuries, others quit because the grind is too much, and others are not good enough to be drafted by the pros. Every major league team scouts the high schools, universities, and baseball leagues in the United States and foreign countries, looking for the best players on planet Earth. In some instances, they believe their prospect is a cut above his peers, and he is offered a signing bonus.

Once management agrees who they will invite to fight for a position on their team, they assign players to their minor league farm system. The most talented players are assigned to the AAA, the less talented are assigned to AA, and the marginal to A. To become a successful organic networker, it is important that you build a farm system that emulates professional baseball. This is where patience comes in. In the minor leagues, players are assigned a variety of coaches – batting, fielding, position, and pitching coaches – to help them improve their skills. The coaches patiently spend hundreds of hours working with the players, and the players must spend hundreds of hours patiently practicing and improving their skills. The reality is that very few minor league players make it to the pros. The system allows moving the most talented players along, until they get their big break.

The difference between our industry and professional baseball is that we open the door to anyone who wants to join our team. Their desire and work ethic to succeed will determine at which level they are placed. As an organic networker, you are responsible for prospecting and recruiting the most talented people to your team. The prospects will start as AAA, AA, or A players. If they are willing to go to work and follow your leadership, they will move through the system and become full-fledged organic network marketing leaders and, in turn, build their own team. You will also sponsor very highly talented, experienced networkers who will immediately be on your starting lineup and bring thousands of distributors with them. Attracting these people to your team will take patience, but it will be time well spent.

To become a successful organic networker, you must have a vision, endurance, and an enormous amount of patience to succeed. In doing so, you will have the opportunity to earn an income and enjoy the lifestyle equal to a professional elite marathon runner or professional major league baseball player, as I have.

Principle #8—Relationships = Communication + Connection

Your ability to build relationships is vital to your success in this industry. The two most important ingredients necessary to become an elite relationship builder are communication and connection. As an organic networker, you will hone your communication skills on several levels. You will use these skills to attract high quality prospects to your organization and then organically connect them into a unified, well-informed, profitable organization.

The power of communication is best exemplified by Johannes Gutenberg, a goldsmith and businessman from the mining town of Mainz, in southern Germany, who borrowed money to build an invention, completed in 1440, that changed the world forever —the replaceable/movable printing press. The printing press had a dramatic effect on European civilization. The printing press made information available quickly and accurately and created a literate reading public that developed an insatiable appetite for knowledge. Most importantly, knowledge became reliable. Using a movable printer, knowledge could be disseminated with an accuracy that could be duplicated over and over. No longer did authors have to worry about errors and inaccuracies that invariably happened when books were tediously copied by hand. Using a printing press gave the common man and scholars the luxury of knowing every word was accurate. It made progress faster and more reliable in business, education, and politics.

Eventually, the printing press would radically alter how people viewed the world and universe. Societies of all types—scientific, political, philosophical, medical, and business—came together and discussed common interests. Soon, these societies crossed international borders and went global, as their common interests knew no boundary. The members of these societies were in the people business, which transcended all geopolitical borders. It is my contention that they were very good network marketers, and the societies took the knowledge that came from their meetings and paid it forward to the world. Sound familiar? The formula was simple: Relationships = Communication + Connection.

Although the world has changed, the importance of communication hasn't. If you are building a network marketing business, you must find a way to become an elite, master communicator. What is so exciting about our industry is that when you marry communication to the advances in technology, it can make you as formidable as any business on Wall Street or in the world. It doesn't matter that you're building a business from your home office that might be located on a rural backwoods farm, mountaintop, small town, or in the shadows of a skyscraper in a metropolitan city. Your ability to compete on a local and global level is at your fingertips. The communication barriers that had existed in the past have been erased. No longer are you confined by geopolitical borders, distance, language, or cultural barriers.

In the 1950s, when the pioneer network marketing companies opened their doors, the leaders had two technologies available to help them build a business – the rotary phone and the automobile. Although those pioneer leaders didn't have the advantages that network marketers have at their fingertips today, they sustained and grew.

Today you have the ability to touch the lives of thousands of people around the globe. To paraphrase what a friend in our industry once told me: To make a million dollars, you need to make a million friends. To do this and pay your success forward, you must connect to the potential leaders you sponsor into your organization. Do not be intimidated by technology. You'll be pleasantly surprised how user-friendly social media, texting, crafting attractive flyers, and advertising via the Internet is. I encourage you to embrace the array of technologies available to you and connect with your downline. Keep them tuned in, build a professional and personal relationship with them, and you will have opened the secret to paying it forward. You get what you give, and everyone benefits.

If you are committed to succeeding in network marketing, then do what every successful networker does—whether it be in network marketing, real estate, the automobile industry, or the local pizza parlor—learn to communicate using every resource available, from technology to the personal touch. Build relationships that turn into lifelong friendships and profitable network marketing partnerships.

One of the reasons I did not succeed in my first network marketing company was my inability to communicate and connect with people. In my second network marketing company, I learned to embrace the communication skills needed to connect with people, and I created a community of network marketers that reached 200,000 strong. By the third company, I was way over a million network marketers.

Principle #9—Wisdom = CANEI + Willingness

My father's goal, since childhood, had always been to become an officer in the Iranian military. After high school, he attended a prestigious military academy, became a high ranking officer, and travelled the world, proudly representing his country. He stayed current on national and international affairs, read everything he could get his hands on to improve his skills, and attended military forums that were in the best interest of his country. In his readings and travels, my father was exposed to Kaizen, which was created in Japan following World War II. Kaizen means, continuous improvement, and was born from the Japanese words *kai*, which means, change, or to correct, and *zen*, which means, good.

The derivative of Kaizen is CANEI (Constant And Never Ending Improvement). CANEI is an evolutionary and organic process that embraces the philosophy that, through the openness and willingness to move forward, an upward spiral is created that will empower our life and personal development. Although CANEI can be applied to all aspects of life, it is tailor-made for the organic networker, because it is one hundred percent focused on you— your personal wants, goals, dreams, and wishes. What is so attractive about CANEI is that, if you want to make a major change in your life, you have to do it by making little changes that eventually accumulate into major and significant life changes. CANEI embraces the idea that it is okay to stumble when you start your business because you can do something every day to get better and better. What makes CANEI so intrinsically organic is that, to be successful in business, you must continually improve every aspect of your personal, social, and business life. There is only one catch to CANEI: the responsibility to improve your life is yours and yours alone.

Unbeknownst to me, my father began teaching me CANEI when I was very young. Like most Iranian boys, I had acquired a love of soccer. Even at a young age, pickup games in the park were fiercely competitive. My father knew how much I loved the game, but before he agreed to help me, he made it clear that improving my skill level was my responsibility, and his responsibility was to provide me the best coaching possible. I wanted my father to teach me how to kick the ball farther than any kid in the neighborhood, which would make me the envy of my teammates.

My father explained that distance meant nothing, if I did not work on the fundamentals required to improve my skills and become a complete player, rather than a one-dimensional player, who could only kick a soccer ball farther than any of my buddies. My father taught me on the physical and the mental level. The physical had to do with learning the fundamentals of ball handling. The mental had to do with strategy. I had multiple goals that I wanted to achieve and, of course, as an impatient young boy, I wanted to achieve them overnight. But I learned through my father that the only way I would improve was to continually work on the fundamentals. Although I was not aware of it at the time, CANEI was becoming hardwired into my DNA.

Like the majority of people who join a network marketing company, I was filled with a lot of hope and promise that my life was about to change, dramatically, for the better. After experiencing my high-tech company, going bankrupt, and losing my house and automobile, I was determined to achieve the lifestyle I had dreamed of for many years. I educated myself on the fundamentals that I would need to succeed. I was determined to become the best-educated student in the industry.

CANEI kicked into high gear the day my mentor and I were headed to an event in Montreal, several hours from my home. I was supposed to drive, but instead I tossed him the keys and asked him to drive. Since I had access to one of the top leaders in my company, I was determined to make the most of learning from him. By the time we reached our destination, I had 80 pages of invaluable notes, specific fundamentals of CANEI that were my responsibility to practice every day to become a top earner in the company.

There is only one catch to CANEI: the responsibility to improve your life is yours and yours alone. Therefore, it is up to you to educate yourself and become a student of the game in order to become a successful organic networker. Why is it that medical doctors, lawyers, university professors, and CEOs of major corporations continually educate themselves? How would you feel if you were admitted to a hospital emergency room and the attending physician hadn't read a book, attended a seminar, or stayed current in his profession since he graduated from medical school? Today, technology is changing so rapidly that in order to survive, professionals need to become the best students of their game or they will perish.

To become a student of the profession of organic networking, I encourage you to become a CANEI sponge. As we all know, a sponge will soak up whatever is around it. The challenge is to not soak up the negative. The fundamentals are available in the training materials of every network marketing company. In addition, every responsible leader designs and provides structured training that focuses on the fundamentals.

Characteristics of a CANEI sponge:

- You are willing to work on the fundamentals daily.

- You never stop learning.

- You have two big ears and one very small mouth. You listen. Never wait for your turn to speak.

- You never wait for the Wizard of Oz to grant your wish.

- You take the wisdom you have acquired and spread it throughout your organization.

- You take in the good and squeeze out the bad.

Principle #10—Leadership = Reliability + Wisdom

How was I able to go from zero to millionaire in eighteen months in my second network marketing company? I focused on leadership.

Early in my networking career, I attended numerous leadership conventions and watched industry superstars and motivational speakers prowl the stage. They shared their story about their backs being against the wall, then joining a network marketing company, going to work, and as the saying goes: *The rest is history.* At the end of their speech, they would look the audience in the eye, and with conviction say the proverbial: *If I can do it, you can do it.* Their speech was inspirational, but their approach was generic. It did not address the wisdom I was searching for, which was: How to become a reliable, successful leader.

I'll be the first to tell you that I am not a motivator. I feel uncomfortable telling an audience: *If I can do it, you can do it.* For me to help people change their lives, I knew I had to come up with an easy-to-follow, reliable, organic leadership blueprint for success.

For me, the principle of leadership began at a very young age. As a kid I became fascinated with electronics and taught myself to design and build circuit boards by developing a reliable, step-by-step process for achieving the intended result. Because of the step-by-step process that I developed, I was able to teach my geek buddies how to design and build circuit boards and, in turn, they were able to teach their friends.

A genuine organic network marketing leader is an entrepreneur, innovator, architect, and trailblazer. Unlike industry leaders or CEOs of corporations, the vast majority of leaders in our industry have not earned an MBA from a prestigious university, are not highly trained, do not move in high-society circles, and are not well connected to power brokers. On the contrary, our industry caters to the masses, that is, people who want to fulfill their dreams and take control of their lives.

In order to become an organic leader, you must first identify your, why, which is the foundation of your business. Then, implement the organic leadership system, which I call the holy trinity of building your business: sponsoring new people, retaining them, and putting money into their bank account. Once you have identified your, why, and implemented your leadership system, you will gain the wisdom and reliability to touch the lives of thousands of people.

Principle #11—Respect = Wisdom + Open-Mindedness

This principle has become paramount, from the day my mother hired my first smuggler to help me escape tyranny to the success I enjoy today. What we have grown to respect in life runs the gamut from respecting what Mother Nature throws at us to hero worship. If you're going to be a successful organic networker and fulfill your wildest dreams, you will have to personally pave the road with respect for yourself, your future leaders, and network marketing as the business that will allow you to achieve the lifestyle of your dreams.

Do not, under any circumstance, underestimate the power of network marketing, and never apologize for your decision to join your network marketing company. Products sold via network marketing contribute billions of dollars to the world economy. Respect the fact that network marketing companies have been a venue for a staggering number of millionaires, who would not have achieved their dreams any other way. Respect the fact that millions of network marketers enjoy benefits, such as luxury automobiles and exotic travel that rival those of any corporate upper echelon or executive in any major company on the planet. Respect the fact that network marketing is as demanding as any business that requires a hefty investment just to get off the starting line. And, in the beginning of your career, respect the fact that you might not do very well, but if you will draw a line in the sand and dare anyone or anything to try to stop you, you will improve and grow. The first thing all prospects will do is look at you and ask themselves: Are you the type of person I respect and want to be in business with? Trust me, they will come to a conclusion within 60 seconds of meeting you.

Equally important is the respect you have for the potential leaders you recruit and the potential leaders they bring to the table. Respect has nothing to do with the luxury car you drive, beautiful home you live in, designer clothes you wear, exotic vacations you enjoy, or the size of your bank account. Respect has to do with your integrity, honesty, leadership, and knowing that your only purpose is to help them grow and become successful.

It is my theory that open-mindedness is the direct route to understanding my principle of Respect. Take every opportunity available to learn about respect, and your biggest opportunity will come via prospecting. From day one, I was laser-focused on prospecting. One of my most rewarding experiences and lessons came in the late '90s when I was leaving my health club and noticed a gift basket of personal care products on a table. A sign taped to a fishbowl read: Drop your business card and win this gift basket. I was impressed with whomever took the initiative to implement this type of prospecting campaign. I dropped my business card in the bowl, knowing that this person was definitely going to follow up. More importantly, I was determined to have her join my team.

A couple days later, the gift basket lady called me, and after two hours on the phone, we agreed to meet for coffee. She was a highly successful leader in another company. When she agreed to leave her company and join my team, I gained wisdom about how to work with women, which has been invaluable throughout my career. Let's face it, women make up the lion's share of network marketers in the world.

While my role model was my mother, working with this woman gave me the wisdom and respect that women bring to network marketing. They are fiercely proud of the company they represent and treat their business as though they had invested $250,000 to get started. At the pinnacle of my worldwide growth, 65 percent of my organization was composed of women. In every country where

I have built an organization, I have learned that women are terrific multi-taskers and highly organized. They pay attention to the fundamentals, have a wide range of friends, and have built a network to become the most prolific social networkers on the planet.

I use women as an example, but the bottom line is that respect will serve you well if you are open-minded and use the wisdom that flows in your direction.

Principle #12—Humility = Values + Self-Awareness

To implement this principle, you will need to assess your values and self-awareness in terms of an honest view of your own personality and your ability to interact with others, frankly and confidently. In the beginning, your potential leaders will look to you for leadership, as you have assured them that you are the go-to person they can rely on to help them achieve their dreams. In the years that I have been in this great industry, I have heard speakers say: To succeed, we must put the needs of others before our own. This statement is multi-dimensional, in that humility, in relation to network marketing, is deeply rooted in a positive value system and a self-awareness of our strengths and weaknesses.

An organic network marketer is aware of his strengths and weaknesses and is willing to work on and continually improve them in order to achieve his goals. No one can be everything to a business or to a relationship. We all start in this business with rough edges. The good news is that network marketing offers an asset that is unheard of in any other industry, which is: By helping others, everyone wins. For example, your potential leader may be weak at prospecting but is willing to do whatever it takes to improve. By using your strengths as an excellent prospector to mentor your leader, it is a win-win situation.

It has been my experience that if network marketers have their business values in place, put others first, and have a self-awareness of who they are and what they are capable of accomplishing, there is no need for ego. Humility is a far better trait.

In an organic garden, as in an organic business, everything, from the treatment of the soil to the planting of the vegetables, plays an intricate role in the health and success of the harvest.

Mentors, in both business and personal relationships, touch us in many ways. The mentor who has had the most influence on my life is my angel uncle. Putting my needs before his own and taking the risk of being arrested and executed, he arranged and paid for a smuggler to take me to Turkey. When I was arrested and sent to a maximum-security prison, he worked tirelessly to locate where I was being held and made arrangements to secure my release. Had the authorities realized he was responsible for hiring my smuggler, he most assuredly would have been executed. My point is, although he is worth millions of dollars, today, given the same circumstance, he would put me first and his wealth second. The humility and respect with which he treats family, friends, and business associates is the model I try to incorporate into my business and personal life every day.

ORGANICWISE:

You now have my *12 Organic Principles for Success* under your belt. They were born from my journey to escape tyranny and live in freedom, to being imprisoned, to arriving in Greece without a penny to my name. Yet, twenty years later, I have fulfilled every dream I had ever envisioned. Now, the second part of my dream – Pay it forward.

The biggest reward goes to the people who are determined to change their lives in a positive way.

In organic networking, you are the CEO of your own destiny.

Chapter 2

WHY ORGANIC NETWORKING?

A good friend once called network marketing the last bastion of free enterprise for anyone seeking to achieve above-average financial results. I agree with him in principle. My perspective has a positive twist: When supported by my 12 Organic Principles for Success, organic networking is the new frontier for free enterprise on a global scale.

Network marketing is a business that will compensate you on two levels: (1) on personal sales you generate and sales generated by the people you recruit and (2) on your leadership ability to help people in your business build teams that can generate hundreds of thousands of dollars in sales per month and receive a residual income that can provide you the lifestyle of your dreams.

Organic Networker has been crafted from my life's journey and network marketing experience. My theory is that everything in life is organically connected. I believe that a true organic networker must learn to integrate and continually improve all three aspects of their life—business, personal, and social—to achieve success and the lifestyle of their dreams. Therefore, my *12 Organic Principles for Success* will help you focus and become successful in all aspects of your life, including network marketing.

When I was first introduced to network marketing, I was attending Carleton University in Ottawa, Canada, majoring in engineering. Engineering seemed to be a part of my genetic code, since I began designing and building circuit boards when I was nine years old. But, rather than take notes and listen to the professor, I would sit in the lecture hall and dream of owning and building my own business. I would envision what my business looked like and the lifestyle I would enjoy.

The reality of launching my own business didn't look promising because of my hefty course load, and I had to financially support my mother and myself, working two part-time jobs. I got involved selling vacuum cleaners, but after zero sales in six months, I had to admit I was not destined for success as a door-to-door salesman. My second part-time job was stocking shelves in a computer store where I met Super Dave, who, at twenty-three, was earning significant extra income in a network marketing company. In spite of his enthusiastic pitches, the picture he painted seemed too good to be true. But, I admit, the reason I didn't join was because I was afraid of what he would think of me if I failed.

The profession touched my life a second time when my mother told me about two brothers who were making good money in a business that they ran out of their basement. I've always been a very practical guy, and building a business out of my basement didn't hit my hot button. Besides, I strongly believed that I needed a university degree to be a successful entrepreneur. Fortunately, my mother was persistent, and I agreed to explore what those basement-business tycoons were up to. Unlike my prior encounter with Super Dave, I was ready to move past my fear and explore the extraordinary opportunities in network marketing.

Enter the New Frontier

It's amazing how a single decision can make all the difference. I was already aware that traditional employment would limit my ability to make money. After all, I would be completely dependent on annual raises, potential year-end bonuses, and job promotions. A commission-only sales job offered independence and opportunity. But I had to support my mother and myself, and without sales, there would be no income. I wanted the freedom to make money, lots of it, without any of the typical restraints that come with being employed by someone else.

While some may challenge this statement, no other profession has created as many success stories as network marketing. Over the past five decades, great network marketing companies have enabled hundreds of thousands of distributors to earn millions of dollars. They have also helped millions of people around the world earn an additional income stream. When I talk with people who are exploring opportunities in my business, I always tell them, "Don't be part of the world economy; instead, create your own economy!"

The opportunity to create your destiny is the freedom to be found in organic networking. It is one of the only enterprises available in the world today where an average person can create an above-average lifestyle. There is no glass ceiling. I started out as an immigrant with no degree or professional credibility. Yet, I was determined to make the opportunity work for me. Against all odds and despite all the challenges that I faced during my first few years, I prevailed and became extremely successful.

I use myself as an example, because I probably would not have made it this big in any other profession. Organic networking offers a true level playing field. One of my mentors told me, "Regardless of your race, religion, gender, heritage, or education level, you start on the same level as everyone else in this profession.

The earning potential is limitless, if you are ready and willing to do what is necessary."

Punch Your Own Time Clock

Most of us have endured a boss, whose unreasonable demands on our time were painful and even impossible to manage, and employees would have to juggle every minute of every day, struggling to keep some balance in their lives.

Back when I worked the night shift at a hotel, I was tied to a time clock. No punch, no paycheck – it was that simple. Today, I have the flexibility to adjust my schedule on a daily basis to meet the needs of my business, personal, and social life. The priorities I set are the only objectives that matter.

An important extension of the time flexibility in organic networking is the ability to run your business from your home. For years, I rode the bus to and from work, wasting valuable hours commuting as I earned a living. Now, my daily commute consists of the time I spend walking from my bedroom to my home office, with a pit stop in the kitchen along the way.

Build Locally, Nationally, and Globally

When a person gets involved in a business venture, either as an employee or as an entrepreneur, there can be all sorts of geographic restrictions. A salesperson, for example, may have a defined territory, or a certain business may be limited to a specific vertical market or region. Organic networking opens the field, not granting exclusivity to one distributor or a group of distributors in any specific geographic area. From the recruit who joined last week, to the veteran with twenty-years of experience, everyone has an equal opportunity to build relationships and recruit new distributors in any of the geographical areas that the company has chosen to support.

In addition, as your team of distributors grows, you can often convince your company to expand its reach into new markets. This is Organic Principle #5—Initiative in action and something I have done in the past. In 1997, I met a Thai woman at a computer store who eventually led me to expand my company into Thailand a year later. It all started with simple product sharing, which led me to Bangkok, a few months later, where I built that market through her family and friends.

Help Others

When I started writing this book, I thought about the many people who helped my mother and me, as we made our way from the madness of the Iranian revolution to our new life in Canada. Their warmth and generosity gave birth to Organic Principle #8— Relationships and the pay-it-forward energy I bring to all of my relationships. Organic networking is a pay-it-forward business like no other.

Many highly-acclaimed networking leaders mentored me when I was starting out. Some of the skills I present in this book come from the wisdom they shared. Their professional generosity reminds me that each and every day I must extend my help to others in my business. Regardless of one's background or circumstance, given the support of successful leaders that are willing to pay it forward, anyone can make their dreams come true in this industry.

Collect for Life

With a section title, Collect for Life, you are probably wondering if I am going to discuss an annuity or a lottery payout plan. On the contrary, it has been my experience, if you focus on building your organic network marketing business with the right plan in place, you can capitalize on your initial smart years. Based on the hard work and dedication you put in during your first 18 to 24 months, you can end up financially collecting for life.

You might be shaking your head, at this point, and wondering if I have a screw or two loose. The truth is that, time and time again, I have seen many average individuals get to work and then reap the rewards of their efforts for a lifetime. I have been able to experience this firsthand, before the age of 40 and not once, but twice.

ORGANICWISE:

A network marketing business is built organically, one customer at a time. It's one of the only professions where you can start from scratch and grow to whatever size business you want. Growing your business is a lot like caring for a new tree. You plant the young cutting and tend to it. A year passes, and it's growing a little. Then a couple more years pass, and you have a hearty sapling. Finally, somewhere in the fifth year, you have a mature tree that offers shade or fresh fruit or just a fun place for your kids to climb and dream. And the tree keeps growing.

During the first four years, a tree is developing a strong, intricate root system that will support the immense size it will attain. You can't see the roots growing because they are hidden underground. In the early years of growing your business, you may feel like you're not producing results. Don't give up; the root system is developing! Eventually, you will experience massive growth.

Enter the Positive Zone

Organic networking is your entrée into the Positive Zone of our business. You are in control of your destiny. No one is ever going to fire you, and highly talented, successful mentors will walk with you every step of the way. Of course, given the fact that you run your own business, only you are accountable for your success. To make the experience positive, implement my *12 Organic Principles for Success* and get plugged in.

The net effect of getting plugged in and staying plugged in to the organic process is that individuals typically become very positive and self-motivated. For me, their positive attitude is the motivation to continue building new relationships. Contrast this to a traditional job, where coworkers don't always share the same passion for completing the tasks at hand.

Let's be honest. Most of us want to be around positive people who care. You will find the motivated, achievement-oriented coworkers you are looking to associate yourself with in organic networking.

Relative Risk

Every day we hear stories about businesses closing their doors or people losing their jobs after years of service. No job or position seems to be secure in today's tough economic environment. If I told you that you could lock in your future in such a way that you felt secure, would network marketing be something you would at least consider? Absolutely!

Each year, thousands of entrepreneurs launch new businesses while thousands of other business people close their doors. There is obvious risk involved in being in business for yourself. I learned a long time ago that the greater the risk, the greater the potential return.

On the upside, you are the CEO of your own destiny, the start-up investment is typically minimal, and you will be joining an organization that offers valuable training and support with one goal in mind—your success. On the downside, you will be left to manage your own time and efforts, which I will turn into a positive experience as you work your way through each chapter of this book. In network marketing no one will guarantee you a regular hourly wage or salary. The biggest reward goes to those who stay committed to their goals—the people who are determined to change their life in a positive way.

Coming Full Circle

When I met the two brothers who ran their network marketing business out of their basement, they were selling a juice that helped control allergies. I had suffered from allergies most of my life. I tried the product and it worked; my allergies diminished in severity. With a personal testimonial in hand, I joined the company and spent the next five years learning everything I could about the profession.

I made very little money during that time, for reasons that will become clear in the chapters that follow. For financial reasons, I decided to put my network marketing ventures on hold and focus my energy and resources on building a software company. When the tech bubble burst, coupled with the disaster that struck the United States on September 11, 2001, my new business felt the ripple effect and soon went under.

I was pretty much broke and fully aware that I had to get up, dust myself off, and get moving again. I was weighing my employment options, when I received a phone call that changed my life. The caller was a friend who told me that I had to check out a new company in Canada. And that's what I did. It was—you guessed it—a network marketing company. When I met the owner and learned about him, his company, and his vision, I knew that the profession and the new business opportunity were right for me.

How did I know the company was right for me? Let's explore that in the next chapter.

Chapter 3

CHOOSING THE RIGHT COMPANY

We are constantly bombarded with choices that come at us from every direction and at high speed. TV, radio, email, text, voice-mail, video mail, and social networking notifications can make us feel driven to make quick decisions about purchasing products or joining a network marketing company. Most people who fail in network marketing do so because they get caught in the speed warp and end up in a company with which they are not compatible and are doomed for failure.

As I was writing this chapter, I thought back to when my mother and uncle placed my life in the hands of a smuggler. They had no experience with smugglers-for-hire. But, given the circumstances, they had to move fast, and they selected the first smuggler they met. I was lucky to have survived the results of that quick decision. When it came time to attempt smuggling me into Turkey a second time, my uncle opted to avoid the fast, easy choice of hiring the first smuggler, again, and waited until he found a more reliable smuggler for the job. I made it to freedom without incident due to better planning and the good graces of God watching over me.

Choice, Not Chance

When it comes to selecting a network marketing company, it's never a good idea to leave your decision to chance. I have seen too many network marketers become frustrated with the company they selected. I have also interviewed some of the top leaders and highest income earners in our profession, asking them what, specifically, led them to choose their company. The answers I received were consistent. They did not rely on the *by chance* method, when it came to selecting a potentially life-changing course of action. Instead, they made a strategic, calculated decision by evaluating the options in five key areas. Here's the equation:

Leadership Style + Products + Compensation Plan + Support Systems + Timing = The information needed to choose the right company

Leadership Style

A company's leadership style is very subjective and sometimes the emotional observation that you make as you go through it is what I call, the Organic Evaluation Process. This is the time you spend getting to know your potential company through the actions of the owners and its top leaders. Many companies create an outstanding infrastructure but have no strong leadership team in place to sustain the momentum. By contrast, some companies with good leadership seem to thrive in the face of structural limitations. How can this be?

Consider a talented pianist that plays Beethoven's Concerto No. 5 on a $50,000 Steinway grand piano. Now, if the same pianist were to play on a $2,000 piano, would the Concerto No. 5 still sound beautiful? Absolutely. It's not about the piano; it's about the pianist who has spent a lifetime improving their talent to bring Beethoven's work to life. Similarly, the traits, behaviors, and characteristics of the person or persons outlining the opportunity for you represent a critically important dimension of a company's leadership style. The company itself might not be the Steinway concert grand of infrastructures, but the skills of the leaders make the magic happen. Without this kind of leadership, the likelihood of success with this type of company is limited.

Ultimately, leadership style is about how trust is created within the organization. To paraphrase an old saying: *People don't care about how much you know until they know how much you care.* You can tell a lot about a company by how the leadership team members present themselves and how others perceive them. Great companies have a great field leadership team that contributes to long-term success.

This, of course, connects to Organic Principle #4—Consistency, where the company practices what it preaches, across the board. The leadership team at the top instills great field leadership everywhere it does business. People join the organic networking profession mainly because of the people they know, and they stay in this profession because of the people they meet along the way. A company must have a leadership style that people can relate to and trust.

Take the time to examine the answers to these questions as you evaluate a company's leadership style:

- ❖ What are the backgrounds of the owners and the senior managers?

- ❖ How willing are they to delegate responsibility and encourage input from distributors?

- ❖ Do they have a documented track record of success?

- ❖ Have they managed a network marketing company before, or are they doing it for the first time?

❖ How do they plan to expand globally?

❖ What is the vision of the company, and how is it presented to you? Is it attainable?

A resounding statement that I often share echoes in my mind: *You can predict the future by looking at the past.* This statement is an important consideration when doing due-diligence on a company.

Products

All network marketing companies claim that their products are the next best thing since sliced bread. That makes it essential that you try some of the products and form your own opinion. While some companies do indeed create or have access to innovative products, it is also imperative that the company you choose offers their products on an exclusive basis. The last thing you want to market is a product that turns out to be a repackaged version of something that is currently in the marketplace under a different brand name. Another important factor to consider is whether the company has all the necessary approvals to market the products on a global basis and in each country they target.

In general terms, the best products are those that are:

❖ 100 Percent Consumable: This is a product that a customer will eat, drink, apply to their body, or is a service they pay for on a monthly basis.

❖ Instantly Gratifying and Emotionally Satisfying: Consuming or using the product will make the customer experience gratification and emotional satisfaction.

❖ Unique: You want a product that attracts attention and is consumed because of its special, innovative, cutting-edge qualities.

- ❖ Competitively Priced: When compared to similar products, the price point of the product is reasonable and not inflated.

- ❖ Marketable: You must be convinced that the product has consumer acceptance and will be very easy to market.

- ❖ Scientifically Sound: Scientific research and peer reviews available; credible documentation.

Compensation Plan

Every industry leader I have spoken with had their favorite compensation plan. In general terms, a good compensation plan should meet the following criteria:

- ❖ Designed by Distributors for Distributors. This type of plan supports a high-percentage distributor payout versus a compensation plan that is designed to maximize company profit, often to the disadvantage of the distributor. The plan must reward distributors fairly, regardless of their position within the company hierarchy.

- ❖ Supports a High Distributor Retention Rate. Companies often set the monthly minimum product purchases at a prohibitive level. This will often discourage distributor retention. After a few months, distributors who haven't started building their business watch as their inventory piles up with no return on their investment. Soon, feeling frustrated and disenchanted, they decide to drop out of the program. A compensation plan that has a reasonable cost for the monthly minimum product purchase, commonly known as autoship, will always promote a high retention rate.

- ❖ Pays to Infinity. Some plans have restrictions on the permissible number of pay levels on which a distributor can earn income. In some extreme cases, when a distributor's organization size reaches a certain level, his or her genealogy, the family tree of one's downline, is broken away from the distributor hierarchy. And not just the people leave; the commissions migrate to the breakaway group, as well. An ideal compensation plan should reward the distributor for all activities in his or her distribution hierarchy and continue to pay to infinity.

❖ Offers an Understandable and Transparent Business Volume or Personal Volume Conversion. It is common for network marketing companies to assign a business volume (BV) or personal volume (PV) to the value of items sold. For example, an item selling for $100 may have a BV or PV of 80. The company will then pay the distributor, based on a percentage of the BV or PV.

Look at the following examples and see how the percentage paid can be changed to correspond with a reduction in the BV or PV:

Example: Company A

Goods Value Sold	$1000
BV or PV Conversion	850
Commission Paid	5%
Distributor Commission	$40.25

Example: Company B

Goods Value Sold	$1000
BV or PV Conversion	650
Commission Paid	6.55%
Distributor Commission	$40.25

With different PV or BV and a variable commission rate, the net result is the same. Often, a higher commission rate is set to appear more attractive to the distributor, with an offsetting reduction in the BV or PV conversion. To benefit from these aspects of the compensation plan, be aware of the differences and how the information is packaged.

Going Global, Seamlessly

As more companies pursue global expansion, this aspect of compensation plans is becoming exceedingly more important. A few years ago, it was common practice for companies to require their distributors to reregister as a new distributor in every country that was part of the expansion plan. Not only is this cumbersome for the distributor, it also creates financial issues from many unique perspectives. For example, foreign earnings, currency conversion, varying country tax laws, and other regulations can dramatically increase the complexity of building a global business.

A more progressive business model permits distributors to build a global business from the comfort of their home office, with no concern for the complexities of each foreign entity. The company handles all the foreign regulations and has systems in place to track the distributor's global business, regardless of the country.

In turn, the distributor gets paid on all activities, based upon the rules and regulations of the compensation plan, and earns commissions in the currency of the country in which they originally activated their business. Companies that can offer this type of seamless, worldwide compensation plan will be better positioned as global trade becomes more prevalent.

Centered on Scalability

Scalability relates directly to the income goals of the distributor. You will want to know if the compensation plan has the diversification and flexibility needed to satisfy the low-, medium-, and high-income earners. To achieve scalability, a compensation plan must have a diverse selection of income components that equate directly to a variety of income objectives.

To be scalable-centered, a compensation plan will offer:

❖ Retail Profit: This is the profit paid to distributors on direct retail sales or Internet shopping cart sales.

❖ Team Sales Commission: You receive a percentage commission on the total sales in your distributor network.

❖ Quick Start Sponsorship Bonus or Commission: A bonus or percent commission is paid on the recruitment of new distributors in a defined period of time in order to quickly yield a return on investment.

❖ Team Building Bonus or Commission: You receive a bonus or percent commission on the total number of active distributors in the genealogy of the sponsoring distributor.

❖ Bonus or Commission on Sponsorship: This is a direct bonus or commission for bringing more distributors into the organization.

❖ Trip and Car Incentives: Some companies offer these additional incentives to build loyalty to the company.

The best way to evaluate a plan is to meet and interview the most successful people in the company you are considering. They will be happy to share the benefits of their plan, and you can ask them about the information I've included in this section. Ultimately, your goal in choosing a company is to find the best fit for you and your future. The compensation plan is only one-fifth of that equation.

Support Systems

As mentioned earlier, a good company will have a comprehensive plan in place for going global. Rapid expansion on a global basis requires *support systems* that keep pace with the local ethnic culture. They must also represent a crystal-clear understanding of the legal requirements in every country where business is conducted.

SIDEBAR: THE BEST PLATFORM

A comprehensive technology platform has to be in place before a company goes global, including:

- ❖ Multilingual Capabilities

- ❖ Multicurrency Capabilities

- ❖ Personalized Website Duplication

- ❖ Real Time Business Tracking

- ❖ Social Networking Compatibility

- ❖ Training Systems

Timing

Timing is a critical component of any decision in life. As an organic networker, there are two potential factors that affect your choice to join a company: your personal timing, and the timing of the network marketing company under review.

Personal Timing

In today's fast-paced environment, we often find ourselves struggling to balance a variety of time-related demands. Family, friends, work, hobbies, relaxation, and exercise all require chunks of our time and skillful juggling of the minutes and hours of each day. As you consider adding a network marketing business into the mix, ask yourself: How will I find the time?

The, how, is found in the attitude of the burning desire you feel when you are prepared to make whatever sacrifices or adjustments are necessary to achieve a goal. Organic Principle #10—Leadership will help you identify the, why. This motivating force has to be so important that you will make your network marketing goal a higher priority than other activities. When that inner voice tells you that it's okay to watch TV instead of make cold calls, you buckle down and do what you need to do.

Experience has shown me that many people get involved in network marketing with good intentions. When faced with a list of new and potentially uncomfortable activities, fear drives them to follow a familiar path of least resistance. There is nothing wrong with this. They simply have not reached the right time in their life for the fabulous opportunity before them. Their personal timing is not conducive to making the decision to build an organic networking business.

As that youngster crossing the mountains, I was laser-focused on one thought: reuniting with my mother in Turkey. Did I have a burning desire? Without question! Similarly, when I lost my high-tech company after 9/11 and couldn't find another job, did I have a burning desire to start earning an income? You bet! The timing was perfect when the right network marketing opportunity came along. I approached it with the same intensity and passion as I did with my other ventures and went on to make millions of dollars. And I made sacrifices along the way to ensure that I dedicated the necessary time to realize my own, why.

Personal timing is about the choices we must make in our lives in order to realize our goals and ambitions. The more we desire to attain a goal, the more likely we are to adjust our personal timing to achieve the results we want.

ORGANICWISE:

Choose a company that has plans to grow organically, building momentum over time, rather than making it big overnight. A good company also creates a systematic coordination of its parts, such as a marketing budget with short- and long-range plans; a cohesive strategy for expanding overseas, and financial backing for stormy times.

Company Timing

Mary, a corporate executive, gets a phone call from a friend who gushes that he received the stock tip of a lifetime. He tells Mary that she'd better buy now, before the price goes through the roof. Mary hesitates, because this guy is always into some get-rich-quick idea. She decides to let it go, and the next day the stock doubles in price.

The city where John lives has some vacant lots that are so undesirable that the city can't give them away. One day, he hears rumors that a new re-zoning plan may soon put a new school and shopping mall in the area. John rushes in and buys one lot. Three months later, the city announces that the property doesn't offer enough pluses for a new development. John got that plot of land for next to nothing, and that's exactly what it is worth.

What do these examples have in common? Both Mary and John lacked the right timing and the information needed to support a good decision. You want to be sure that the company under consideration is positioned to grow and succeed and that it has not passed its best-before date. The big companies in network marketing, like major players in other industries, will go through the following four stages of growth:

Stage 1: Creation

- ❖ Inception: This is when a network marketing company is born. An idea and a company come to life.

- ❖ Launch: The foundation, company structure, initial management team, and product development are put into place, and the compensation plan is created.

When sales exceed $10 million per year, the company starts to shift into the second growth stage of expansion.

Average time: 6 to 18 months

Stage 2: Expansion

- ❖ Local expansion: The company begins to closely examine its products, systems, and marketing strategies for their local markets.

- ❖ Global expansion: At this point, the company has started to expand outside of their local markets. Today, this works a bit differently than it did 20 years ago. Today, companies tend to expand globally by following the sales. The former strategy was to look for new markets, which is typical of corporate business expansion plans.

When annual sales exceed $50 million, a major transition occurs. The company goes through an exponential growth curve, resulting in a shift to the pre-momentum stage.

Average time: 18 to 36 months

Stage 3: Momentum

❖ Pre-momentum: This is when the number of distributors in the company has quadrupled in size, and the company is showing up on the radar.

❖ In-momentum: The company attracts all sorts of media attention, resulting in global awareness of its brand and products or services.

Average time: 5 to 10 years

Stage 4: Saturation

❖ Post-momentum: The company continues to grow at a low but consistent double-digit rate. The growth rate can be rejuvenated through the launch of new products and expansion into new countries.

❖ Full Maturity: At this stage, the company enters its last phase of growth. Although company growth now slows to a single-digit rate, it has established a massive global footprint. Full stability is reached.

Average time: 15 to 20 years

You will want to determine whether you want to join a company in the earlier growth stages, in order to benefit from the potentially explosive growth on the horizon, or to take a more conservative approach by joining a company in a later phase of sustained growth. The right choice will be the one where your personal timing resonates with the timing of the company.

Learn Before You Leap

I found the perfect fit for me and my, why, with the new company in Canada that my friend told me about. When I joined, it was in the early Creation-Launch stage. During my evaluation, I met with the leadership and thoroughly checked out the products. I studied the details of the compensation plan and understood how the support systems could assist me.

I ultimately made the right decision, at the right time, to take the leap and get involved. I went to work and within five years was able to retire from the profession at the age of thirty-three. In the next chapter, you'll learn how I made that happen.

Chapter 4

GETTING PLUGGED IN

A quick explanation about what I mean by, Getting Plugged In: In general, most network marketing companies have taken the responsibility of saving you thousands of dollars in start-up costs for office space, warehousing, legal, product formulation, office furniture, and their training systems, to name a few. Think of your company, products, compensation plan, incentives, upline, and training program as a huge energy source that you must stay plugged in to every day.

Once you've made an informed choice as to which company you will join, the question then becomes: Where do I begin? At this point, I am not talking about setting goals or writing out a prospect list. It's more about taking inventory of your dedication, passion, and commitment, to draw a line in the sand and accomplish your goals—no matter the obstacles and challenges you will face—and whether or not you are in your business for the long haul. Therefore, at this stage you will have to come to terms with how you plan to marry your dedication, passion, and commitment to

Organic Principle #6—Persistence. It will define whether or not you have what it takes to make it as an organic networker. And, most assuredly, you will need to embrace Organic Principle #9—Wisdom, which features CANEI.

As stated many times throughout this book, becoming a successful organic networker is about your willingness to patiently and consistently do the work necessary to achieve success in the short term, that will ensure you long-term success.

When I launched my organic networking business, after the demise of my high-tech company, I plugged in and stayed plugged in to my network marketing company until I reached my goals. In the beginning, my passion was so intense that I had one thought running through my mind from the minute I woke up to the moment I fell asleep at night: the vision of how the success of my company would change my life for-ever. I can still remember going to bed and explaining the compensation plan to my potential superstars in my sleep.

This single mindedness can be summed up in Organic Principle #5—Initiative. A thought or idea by itself can give you a temporary feeling of inspiration, but initiative is what gets you through when the perspiration is pouring down your forehead and you have to overcome the inevitable roadblocks and disappointments that come with building a successful business.

Now, take a few minutes to think about and take inventory of your passion and commitment. Are they strong enough to help you achieve your most important goals?

- ❖ How committed are you to achieving these goals? I mean, is the fire of your passion so intense that you are fearless?

- ❖ Under what conditions would you give up and throw in the towel? If there is a single reason that would drive you to quit before you achieve your most important goals, throw in the towel before you start.

❖ What if you could significantly increase your desire to achieve these goals by getting plugged in?

❖ Do you believe that you possess the character to back up what you wish for?

❖ Do you believe that success and a dream lifestyle can become a reality, or is it just a dream for the privileged few?

I knew I was 100 percent committed to my goals when I moved from the dreaming stage, through the passion and commitment stage, and stood before an audience and told them that I knew I was fully committed and plugged in to my company, and my company was plugged in to me. Trust me when I say that there is no stronger synergy than getting plugged in to a company that you are 100 percent convinced provides the opportunity you have always dreamed about. With this mindset, quitting will never be an option. The next step is to write your *Organic Blueprint for Success*, draw a line in the sand, and go to work.

Getting Plugged In—Action Steps

❖ **Step 1. Never Throw in the Towel.** When your goals really matter to you, you quickly understand that, if you quit, you must look that person you have disappointed the most in the mirror every morning—you. To back up your commitment, do yourself a favor and take a stand of courage. But if what I am about to suggest keeps you on track until you succeed, even your detractors will applaud you.

I know that you may have heard this a dozen times, but I want you to share it with everyone who will listen. You are going to quit your job. Most will think you are nuts, joking, or just blowing smoke. Write a letter of resignation and place it in a file on your computer, with a reminder on your calendar. When the day arrives for you to quit your job, attach the letter to an email and send it to your boss. Taking this step may seem a bit scary, because it leaves you no escape route. My point is, you are either committed or not. If you do this, do you think anyone will question your commitment?

Let's face it, when the going gets tough, as it inevitably does to achieve any worthwhile goal, most of us will want to quit. If you find yourself thinking your business is too difficult because too many people are saying, no, to listening to your professional presentation, remind yourself that average people would quit, but since you are not average, the word, quit, doesn't exist in your vocabulary.

❖ **Step 2. Compose a Dream Board.** Let's say that two important goals you have written are to earn a $10,000 monthly bonus by the end of your second year and take that fabulous dream vacation. You need to visually announce your intentions to the world. Write and date a bonus check for $10,000 as if your company wrote it. Make copies of it. The date will correspond with the date that you will indeed receive a check for that amount. Then, find photos of your dream vacation. Post the copies of the faux bonus check and the vacation photos in strategic locations around your house and on your mobile lock screens as daily reminders. Chart your monthly progress. Show and tell everyone your goals. You will be pleasantly surprised at how many people will become interested in your business.

Actor Jim Carey, before he headed for Hollywood, wrote his father a check for $10 million and told him he'd call when he could cash it. Jim had been living in a station wagon, homeless. How many people do you think laughed in his face or snickered behind his back when they heard about the check he wrote to his father? Who do you think had the last laugh when Jim called his father, telling him to cash the check?

* **Step 3. Find Your Cheerleaders.** This falls under Organic Principle #8—Relationships. Have you ever heard cheerleaders in front of a crowd of thousands of fans yell: "We're going to lose! We're going to lose! Go team!" Of course not. On the other hand, many networkers run into a negative tsunami that can douse the flame of their passion. As the old saying goes: *Birds of a feather flock together.* My question to you is, which flock do you think you should join?

When you first join your company, most of your cheerleaders will be your upline and people you meet at opportunity meetings and regional or national conferences. Not only will these people be your cheerleaders, they will share everything they are doing, or have done, to achieve success. When you share your goals with these people, they will encourage you to set the bar even higher! Many will become lifelong friends.

SIDEBAR: LIKE MINDS

Many promising organic networkers drown in the negative tsunami because they listen to the wrong people before they have an opportunity to succeed. It's up to you to associate yourself with a tsunami of cheerleaders that will help and applaud you along the road to success.

Take the responsibility of deleting the negative from your life, whether it is people, movies, or TV. If you are passionate and committed to your goals, this will be a relatively easy decision. When Bill Gates, Steve Jobs, and Mark Zuckerberg were on fire, building their corporations, how many negative people do you think they tolerated for longer than a nanosecond?

In 2001, when I closed my high-tech business and returned to network marketing, I made the conscious decision to delete from my life the people who were not my cheerleaders. My goal was to create a brighter future for my family and myself, and there was no way that negative people would help me achieve my dream. One of my closest friends, whom I had hung out with since high school, constantly discouraged me from getting involved in my network marketing company and encouraged me to stick with my steady, boring job. Although we were running mates, I knew that I was going to have to make a dramatic change in my life in order to succeed, and I could no longer afford to hang out with him and his negativity.

❖ **Step 4. Become a Student of the Game.** It is vital that you embrace the fact that there isn't a profession on earth that doesn't require staying plugged in to the latest literature, industry magazines, trends, breakthroughs, techniques, journals, and attending seminars, conferences, workshops, training courses, and license updates. In reality, the real professionals remain on top of their game throughout their entire career. Remember the CANEI philosophy: *Continual improvement and success is 100 percent your responsibility.* Ask your upline leader to recommend books to read and motivational materials to listen to and add to your library, and then devour them.

Do not limit yourself to reading books that are strictly targeted at network marketing. Read the amazing stories about the incredible struggles Tom Monaghan went through to make Domino's Pizza the success it is today; how McDonald's founder Ray Kroc revolutionized the franchise industry; how Fred Smith took an idea that his university professors thought was totally unworkable, FedEx, and turned it into a billion-dollar industry. Read how Lee Iacocca moved through the ranks of auto engineering, to sales and marketing, and made his way to launching the revolutionarily designed Mustang, which then lead him to become the CEO of Chrysler Corporation.

An amazing transformation takes place when you become more knowledgeable about what it takes to build your organic network marketing business. You will become more confident knowing that you made the right professional choice. In a very short period of time, with the proper work ethic, your confidence will translate into success, and those who have tried to discourage you will begin to understand and admit that you will succeed in spite of their negativity, and many will become your biggest fans.

Do what I do. Feed your mind with some form of motivational material—books, articles, and audio programs—for at least fifteen minutes a day, as inspired by Organic Principle #4—Consistency. This will recharge your batteries and keep your burning desire strong.

ORGANICWISE:

In order to accomplish your goals, proceed with your end in mind. There are no shortcuts in an organic process. Every step, big or small, plays a huge role in achieving your success.

❖ **Step 5. Bad In—Bad Out.** Take a minute and think about all of the sensory inputs that affect your attitude. What do you read? What do you watch on TV? How clean and orderly is your home? Are you constantly barraged by loud music? Once you identify the negative inputs, strive to replace them with positive ones.

I learned, long ago, to be selective about my media inputs. Think of entertainment as fitting into two categories that will feed your mind: organic or junk food. The choice is yours. You can choose the junk food variety that is toxic and will derail any plans you have for achieving your goals, or you can chose the organic variety that will enrich every part of your life.

The bottom line is that you can take everything negative in your life and transform it to positive. Think of it as spring cleaning for success. Whatever is messy—clutter in your office, on your computer, your bedroom, game room, yard, garage, or car—clean it up!

❖ **Step 6. Dress for Success.** When I was attending university, long hair, earrings, and hip-funky clothes were my dress code of the day. The funkier I dressed, the better I liked it. When I became serious about fulfilling my dreams as an organic networker, I could not visualize myself wearing hip-funky clothes. I immediately understood that, if people were going to take me seriously, I needed to dress for success. I dumped the hip-funky clothes, earrings, and cut my hair. I couldn't afford a closet packed with new suits, but as my business grew and I started earning bonus checks, I added professional attire to my wardrobe. Little by little, I created the success identity that was a clear statement of a leader on the rise.

Here is a simple exercise that may sound a little corny but will be well worth your time and effort. Stand in front a full-length mirror and take inventory of the person looking back at you. Then ask yourself if you are dressed as though you were going to present your business opportunity to a room full of people. My point is that you must plug in to Organic Principle #11—Respect, which reminds us that respect has to do with your integrity, honesty, leadership, and knowing that your only purpose is to help them grow and become successful. It is critical that the person you are looking at in the mirror understands that you must be a leader in both appearance and character.

❖ **Step 7. Be a CANEI Sponge.** Organic Principle #9—Wisdom, reminds us that the Japanese philosophy CANEI is a never-ending process of learning and that success is our personal responsibility. Without question, the greatest teachers are also the best students. The day you stop learning is the day you stop growing, both personally and in business. Regardless of your background, education level, or age, you must be a huge sponge that absorbs and learns every day. After close to two decades in organic networking, I'm still learning new techniques and ideas from successful people in the profession.

To be a CANEI sponge you must adhere to the following rules:

❖ Do not question the feedback, training, mentoring, or pointers given to you by a successful leader.

❖ It is your responsibility to take notes and ask questions that will clarify such things as how to properly approach a prospect.

❖ Constantly ask your upline to evaluate your progress.

❖ Take copious notes at training, opportunity, regional, and national meetings.

❖ Embrace the idea that the more you learn, the more you earn.

❖ The more you learn, the more you distance yourself from failure.

❖ Don't try to reinvent the wheel.

❖ Take time every day to wring out the bad and retain the good.

❖ Invite your leaders to be a huge CANEI sponge, as you are.

❖ **Step 8. Goals and Persistence.** Organic Principle #6—Persistence, reminds us that you must have a vision of where you are and where you want to go, and the willpower to fulfill your dreams. There are two fundamental conditions for true persistence. The first involves a solid set of beliefs. As an old saying goes: *Stand for something, or you'll fall for anything.* That's why my *12 Organic Principles for Success* are so invaluable to me, as they let the world know what I stand for. The second condition involves the fact that my behavior must match my character. Combine these two conditions and you end up with a formidable ally: persistence and willpower with a purpose. This combination has been responsible for the careers of many successful business people.

Persistence must become a part of your everyday life. You have to write your short-term, medium-range, and long-term goals. The benchmark as to whether you have the persistence to turn your goals into reality, on a scale of one to ten, must be a ten in all three categories of goals. My contention is that when you write your goals, they must be clearly etched in your mind, and you will not be satisfied until you have achieved them.

Persistence is also tied directly to Principle #10—Leadership. As an organic networker, you must persist in and be committed to your personal goals and dreams and the goals and dreams of the people in your business. Your commitment to them and to yourself must be fulfilled.

Persistence and a burning desire to succeed are common denominators found in all organic networkers who reach the highest levels of success. If you dream about reaching millionaire status, know that it will require at least five years of commitment at full throttle. Although there are very few exceptions to this rule, the majority of millionaires in our profession are average, hardworking people who have committed to at least 10,000 hours to reach mega success. Here is the breakdown:

8 hours a day x 5 days a week x 52 weeks a year x 5 years = 10,400 hours

A part-time organic networker, working 20 hours a week, will invest at least 10 years to reach millionaire status.

As driven as I am, I believe in setting realistic expectations. If your financial goal is to make millions, you need to understand the time commitment to achieve that goal. Does the idea of 5 years, full-time, sound scary? Think about it. You can spend five years at a job, waiting for annual raises or stock options to vest. You can even spend 10,000 hours dreaming about the life you want to live. Or, you can commit to the time needed to achieve real financial wealth.

Whether you make the commitment or walk away, in five years you'll fulfill the destiny you set for yourself. Mark Twain wrote: *Twenty years from now you will be more disappointed by the things you didn't do than by the ones you did do. So throw off the bowlines. Sail away from the safe harbor. Catch the trade winds in your sails. Explore. Dream. Discover.*

❖ **Step 9. Keep Your Eye on the Ball.** Many new networkers who come from or have a structured job can become distracted quite easily. My suggestion is that you become intimately acquainted with Organic Principle #3— Organization. You need to be organized and pay attention to details. If you currently work for someone else, do you play games on your computer, listen to sporting events or music on headphones, text for hours, run errands, call friends just to shoot the breeze, take a nap, or watch television? If you were to do any or all of these activities at work, you would be in line to receive a pink slip and be looking for your next job.

At the heart of organization is learning and incorporating the discipline to achieve a lifestyle that is currently beyond your reach. Just as you must dress for success, you must accept the challenge of getting what you want out of life by incorporating discipline into your daily routine and eliminating the time bandits. As the old saying goes: There is a time to work and a time to play. Do not let one interfere with the other.

Here are a few suggestions to get you on the proper discipline path:

* Plan your day, including time for business, socializing, friends, family, meals, errands, and leisure.

* Prioritize and do the most important tasks first.

* Do not move to your second-level priorities until you have completed your most important tasks.

* Do not try and commit your daily plan to memory. Commit all tasks to paper.

* Write this note and tape it to your time bandits: Not until you have completed your tasks!

* When you are working your business, your office phone and cell phone should be 100 percent dedicated to making business calls.

* Use caller ID to eliminate calls that will break your concentration.

* Let calls go to your voicemail. You can follow up with the missed calls later.

* If you answer the phone and it's a friend, tell them you'll get back to them at a later time. The priorities on your schedule should be the number of prospecting calls and business presentations you will make per day.

❖ I will absolutely guarantee you that once you learn to keep your eye on the ball, write down the tasks you must complete each day, and develop the discipline to carry them out, you will be blown away by the growth of your business on a daily basis.

❖ **Step 10. Catch Lightning in a Bottle.** Actually, the saying goes like this: *It's like trying to catch lightning in a bottle.* This adage is generally used when describing someone or a sports team that has accomplished what is considered the impossible. To catch lightning in a bottle, to make your dreams come true in network marketing, at times may seem impossible, but it can be done, and you can do it. Unless you win the lotto, achieving the lifestyle you have always dreamed about is going to take work.

The reason that so many people never try to catch lightning in a bottle is because they can't wrap their minds around how to turn their dreams into reality because they aren't willing to do the work necessary to make those dreams come true. The reality is that, to become a successful networker, it is important to understand that everything you do to build your business isn't always exciting. Sometimes the task at hand can feel like pure drudgery. That's why you must be laser-focused on reaching your goals. The fun starts as you accomplish your short-term goals and your bonus checks reach $10,000 per month. Once this happens, all of the hard work fades into a distant memory. You accept the fact that tasks that looked like drudgery are simply the necessary steps you had to take on the road to success.

My suggestion is to take what you initially think of as drudgery and turn it into a positive task.

❖ Learn to love the word, no. Every, no, you receive when prospecting is money in the bank because it puts you closer to a, yes.

❖ Set mini deadlines and complete them as quickly as possible. Challenge yourself by using a timer.

❖ Look in a mirror and smile when making prospecting calls.

❖ Practice your elevator prospecting pitch, as if you were getting on an elevator and going to the top floor with someone. What would you say in that short period of time that would grab their attention to listen to your opportunity?

❖ Take a break every couple of hours and go out for a fifteen-minute brisk walk. When you return to your office, you'll be invigorated and focused on your next tasks.

❖ Before you pick up the phone to make a prospecting call, say to yourself: "(Prospect's name), this is going to be one of the best days of your life!"

These are only a few suggestions. I am certain that, as you settle into the routine of building your business, you can come up with more ways to convert drudgery into a positive.

The bottom line is that the only thing that will allow you to catch lightning in a bottle is hard work. Once you've made a commitment to your business, you need to ask yourself how hard you are willing to work to achieve your goals. Are you willing to commit a certain number of hours to your business every week for the next 18 to 24 months, regardless of the immediate outcome?

Many new network marketers end up quitting within their first 90 days because they can't see the light at the end of the tunnel. I've also seen new distributors come in with an Organic Principle #9—Wisdom mindset and, from day one, faithfully follow their mentors' advice until they reach huge success. There are also new people who make countless mistakes and finally learn to surrender to the wisdom of their mentors, following them step by step to greatness. As you know, doctors study and train for many years before they can open a practice, and then they continue to work with gusto to get paid what they're worth. It's no different with lawyers, accountants, and other professionals, including network marketers.

❖ **Step 11. Sacrifice to Succeed.** One of the most important components of success in this profession: the willingness to sacrifice in order to achieve your goals. Most of us realize this going in. However, before we can make sacrifices, we have to overcome our resistance. How can we make our task easier? How can we reduce the sting? Change your perspective. Take the word, sacrifice, which has a negative connotation, implying that to get something of value we have to put forth an effort that includes a lot of drudgery, and look at the positive connotation of sacrifice.

The willingness to sacrifice is a sign of strong character. While others wait for things to happen, you can make things happen. Many successful people did not take vacations, long weekends, or watch sporting events at the expense of their goals. They put their goals first. Which would you rather do: Work diligently for a few years, so that your family can be in a position to do what they want for the rest of their lives or fall victim to your resistance?

Here's a case in point from my own company. A new distributor started in network marketing shortly after he got married. He and his wife chose to wait to go on their honeymoon until almost two years after their wedding. They not only held off until they could afford a fabulous honeymoon, they also waited until they could afford it from a time perspective. They made a commitment to the people in the company who were committed to their success.

Be prepared to forfeit some temporary, more appealing choices in order to put your goals first and foremost. Stay upbeat, changing course whenever necessary, with your end goal in mind.

❖ **Step 12. Stay Plugged In.** One of my first lessons on the importance of staying plugged in came in the early '90s. One of my leaders was unplugged from what was going on in the company. As a result, he was out of the loop on some of the company's crucial updates. In the short term, this cost him some bonus money. But the long-term effects were far more dramatic. His team had witnessed him unplugging, and many of his downline consciously adopted the same behavior. A year later, his checks had dropped immensely, to the point that he had to look for another job to supplement his income. The importance of staying plugged in is crucial.

Chapter 5

LAUNCHING YOUR BUSINESS

Have you ever looked at your career and asked yourself: "How in the world did I get here?" I surely did, when my high-tech company was rapidly disintegrating before my eyes. I spent hours analyzing how I could get out of that mess. That's when I realized I hadn't been setting any goals. While I had gone through years of schooling, I had never received any training on goal setting.

A turning point for me was when I began setting goals. Goal setting gave me a sense of control that most people never get to experience. I also learned that desires, like making more money or building a business, are not goals in the truest sense. A goal is a specific, clearly defined, measurable state that must be defined in what I call, binary terms. At any point, if I were to ask you if you had achieved your goal yet, you must be able to give me a definitive, yes or no, answer. Maybe is not an option.

Instead of, making more money, a true business goal would be: My additional income is $5,000 or more by January 1. On January

1, when I ask you if you've achieved your goal, you should be able to give me a definitive answer. That is the level of clarity you need.

Along with planning goals in binary terms, be as detailed as possible when setting your goals. Give specific numbers, dates, and times. Make sure that each of your goals is measurable. Also, define your goals as if you already know what's going to happen. I tell people, "The best way to predict the future is to create it."

SIDEBAR: CREATE YOUR FUTURE

Pick a point in the future, whether it's six months from now or five years from now, and spend a few hours writing out a concise description of where you want to be by that time. That sense of knowing what you want isn't going to just come to you in a form of divine inspiration. You have to move toward it and create a story for yourself, backed up by clearly defined goals.

Commit Your Goals to Writing

If you have been waking up each morning and winging it, then ask yourself, "How much longer will I continue to climb the ladder of success, only to realize too late that it was leaning against the wrong building?"

Goals have to be put in writing. Any goal that is not committed to writing is just a fantasy. It is also best if you write your goals as positive, present tense, and personal affirmations. Phrase them as if they are already achieved. Instead of saying, I will earn $70,000 this year, write your goal as, I earn $70,000 this year. If you phrase your goals in future terms, you are sending a message to your subconscious mind to keep your desired outcome in the future, beyond your grasp.

In this new techno-age, I suggest that you create a mobile lock screen as a constant reminder of what you are committed to achieving in life.

Also avoid indecisive words like: probably, should, could, would, might, or may. These words foster doubt as to whether you can actually achieve what you are going after. Choose goals that are meaningful to you. If a goal doesn't feel personally important, you won't make a commitment to the step-by-step process of achieving it.

I am a true believer in the mindset: *If you believe it, you can achieve it.* Before you can believe in a personal goal, you have to first create it in your mind. You have to see yourself in the situation where your goal has already been achieved. Be it a luxurious vacation, a beautiful home, or seeing your kids graduate from a prestigious university, you've got to see it in your mind and believe in its fulfillment.

When I was in college and dreaming about starting my own business, my personal, why, involved my desire to take care of my family, particularly my mother. I used to picture myself handing my mother the keys to a new home that was totally custom-designed to her liking. Although the dream didn't materialize for over a decade, it did eventually turn into a reality. This illustrates the power of your mind. If you envision a goal and really believe in it, anything is possible.

Leap into a Plan of Action

Setting goals is not a passive act. You must take direct, conscious action. Everything counts and nothing is neutral. You are either moving toward your goals or you're moving away from them. You get results only from the physical actions you take, never for the ideas you hoard.

One of the secrets to success is recognizing that motivation follows action. The momentum of continuous action fuels motivation.

Procrastination, on the other hand, kills motivation. So act boldly, as if it's impossible to fail. If you keep adding fuel to your burning desire, you will reach the point of knowing you will never quit. Achieving success is nothing more than a matter of time.

Once you set a goal for yourself, immediately tune in to Organic Principle #5—Initiative. Don't worry about making detailed, long-term goals. People often get stuck in the state of analysis paralysis and never take action. Your plan will develop as you identify the action you need to take to meet your most immediate goals, and then dive in headfirst.

SIDEBAR: CREATE A VISION BOARD

Surround yourself with images of your desired outcomes as already achieved in your mind's eye. That's why a vision board is such a simple, yet powerful tool.

Here is what you need:

- ❖ Foam core board, poster board, or stretched canvas

- ❖ Scissors

- ❖ Glue Stick

- ❖ Old magazines in different genres

Mediocre goals lead to mediocre results.

Cut out pictures and words that match your goals or represent results of your dreams coming true. Place your vision board where you'll see it every day. Update it as goals shift or are accomplished. Don't worry about how the goals will be accomplished. Let your vision board inspire you as you take action. Don't forget to commit your goals to your mobile lock screen on all your devices.

Support Your Goals

Here are some of the action steps that make up the support system for your goals:

- ❖ Decide what you need to focus on in your business in order to achieve your, why.

- ❖ Develop a master list of 100 people to bring to your team and how to invite them. This will be the basis of your present and future pipeline of prospects.

- ❖ Once you sign up your first distributor, identify the next step. How do you get them plugged in to the existing training system so they will be part of your team and help it grow?

- ❖ Read industry-related books and listen to audio trainings.

- ❖ Attend personal-growth seminars.

- ❖ Treat your business as though you had invested $250,000 in it.

- ❖ Learn how to deal with rejection that can come on a daily basis.

- ❖ Connect into the system of the company you joined.

- ❖ Be aware of the resources and contacts you have to build your business.

- ❖ Use technology to present your company through a website and the power of the Internet.

- ❖ Be your #1 customer, a living testimonial for your product.

- ❖ Learn how to introduce and promote your fellow distributors, whom you will rely upon for testimonials and sharing details about your company. Remember that people you know well will often take a third-party validation more seriously than one from you.

❖ If you have access to a system developed in collaboration with your company, then take action and implement Organic Principle #8—Relationships.

System features often include:

❖ Use daily company-provided live and recorded conference calls and webinars. These calls were my best friend in the early days!

❖ Invite prospects to daily live and recorded three-way calls, so they can see that you have a system that is not dependent solely on your word.

❖ Three-way calls with experienced leaders in your company to explain the merits of the company.

❖ Align prospects with upline business partners by connecting people who have mutual interests and backgrounds. Connect a nurse with a nurse, a manager with another manager, an automotive specialist with a car salesperson, etc.

❖ Participate in and attend home and site meetings at hotels or other locations.

❖ Attend annual company conventions. Here, you will continue to lock in your beliefs.

❖ Make every day count. Even small actions done daily will advance your business.

❖ Take massive action when you feel you have the momentum and experience to take your business to the next level.

Goals-in-Progress

Any good plan is a work in progress. There will be times when progress is slow and adjustments are needed. There will be other times when there's real momentum and your efforts start to pay dividends. I have always believed that today's preparation is tomorrow's success—the core of Organic Principle #1— Readiness. When I was building my organic networking business, I saw that the more I prepared each day, the easier it became to achieve my goals. This didn't mean that I spent all my time preparing. Once I had done some prep work, I took action and evaluated the outcome. Time and time again, I repeated this cycle, refining and learning as I gained more experience and success.

Several years ago, I watched the construction of a thirty-story building adjacent to my residence. The construction team put in an immense amount of time measuring and excavating the six-story hole for the foundation. After they secured the foundation, they started building the concrete infrastructure for the base of the skyscraper. Then, over the next 18 months, the building was constructed. About two years later, the building was ready for business.

The project did not provide any revenue to the building developers and owners for over four years. But the developers had a solid plan, grounded in the knowledge that their investment would ultimately pay off with full occupancy. This analogy closely parallels the building of a new organic networking business. Success can be achieved only when you have established a plan of action and have the patience to follow that plan over a period of time.

SECTION TWO

PEOPLE SKILLS

Organic networking involves a network of people.
We connect with men and women from all walks of life,
bringing them into our network and helping them to realize their dreams.

Chapter 6

BUILDING POSITIVE RELATIONSHIPS

Several years ago, partly due to the industry-wide recognition for my accomplishments, I was invited to participate in writing a book about network marketing. I wrote the foreword and contributed many of my professional insights about how to build a successful business. The opportunity was as exciting as it was humbling. One of the upsides to this experience was that I began to understand that much of my success was due to the relationships I had built over the years.

Organic networking involves a network of people from within your organization, to your mentors, to people you will connect with who are in the process of becoming industry superstars. It's about connecting with people from all walks of life, bringing them into our business, and helping them realize their dreams. We not only build our businesses one person at a time, we also build our network one positive relationship at a time. This chapter offers my insights as to how each of us can more effectively build and maintain those positive relationships.

Make the Connection

Throughout our lives, we are exposed to a select few individuals with a significant message to share and an amazing ability to deliver and communicate it. Sometimes their delivery style can be soft-spoken and charismatic, or they communicate dynamically with something more like brute force.

During World War II, when Winston Churchill led his country through formidable challenges, he spoke to the nation about standing strong against the Axis powers. His voice rang out with force, boldness, and conviction of purpose. In stark contrast to Churchill, Nelson Mandela spoke to the world in a gentle, reassuring, and reserved voice. But let there be no mistake, Mandela's messages came across as loud and clear as Churchill's. They had vastly different styles, but they were both great leaders and moved their nation to action.

On the other hand, what about us, the mortals? What about those times that you've been asked to speak or give a presentation but were not as effective as you could have been? You did not connect with the audience, fumbling your speech because of poor communication skills, and then wanting to escape the room as soon as possible. I know I have! At times like this, it takes the power of Organic Principle #7—Patience to stay present and focused. The question becomes: What is it that separates the best from the rest?

An effective delivery style, whether you are speaking to one person or to an audience of thousands, forms a bond between you and the people you are addressing. The good news is that we can learn from those who have mastered this skill and apply this wisdom to both our business and personal relationships.

Speaking to a Group

As I developed my own style of connecting with my audiences, I learned to avoid certain pitfalls that plague many speakers:

- ❖ Never use a monotone voice. Your voice needs energy, or you'll lose their attention.

- ❖ To get feedback, ask yes/no questions.

- ❖ Make eye contact with the audience, to create a sense of connection.

- ❖ Raise the tone of your voice, where it's needed, for impact.

- ❖ Pause for emphasis, before or after a key message.

- ❖ Have fun and enjoy the experience. Your audience will respond in kind.

- ❖ Share a funny story, where it's needed and appropriate.

- ❖ Most importantly, gauge your audience's reaction throughout your speech. The longer you speak in front of people, the more important this awareness becomes.

The Power of a Positive Attitude

Connection starts with one absolutely essential skill: having a positive attitude. This is in line with the relationship-centered Organic Principle #8—Relationships. The right attitude always counts, whether you're dealing in the business world or communicating with family members. We need to display a positive mindset, at all times, and encourage it in others. As a result, people will make two important shifts: they will change their negative thinking, and they will be more willing to accept your perspective about what it takes to build a business.

Of course, it's impossible to avoid negative situations. You might discover that someone has said something unflattering about you. A friend may do something that makes you feel rejected or disappointed, or you may bear the brunt of someone's bad mood. In these situations, it can be difficult to stay positive. You may even find yourself reacting negatively, which often makes the situation worse.

The brilliant scientist Albert Einstein once said, "In the middle of every difficulty lies opportunity." My own motto continues where Einstein left off: Beat the negative situations by staying positive. This is the attitude I applied when I was locked up in the juvenile section of a maximum-security prison. Those days had dark moments, but simple things, like playing games with the other boys and finding joy in the friendships that were created, kept me from sinking into despair.

The next time negativity threatens to take down your upbeat attitude, overpower it with these action steps:

- ❖ Take a slow, deep breath to calm yourself down. If you aren't feeling calm, don't respond.

- ❖ Speak in a gentle voice to reduce the tension of the situation.

- ❖ Examine the other person's message for something positive that you can act on to improve yourself. Ignore anything negative.

- ❖ Maintain a positive perspective of the other person. Maybe you don't like their messages or their behavior, but that doesn't mean you should immediately write them off.

- ❖ Realize that harboring negative feelings will hurt you, not the other person.

- ❖ Admit when you've made a mistake. As George Bernard Shaw wrote: A life spent making mistakes is not only more honorable, but more useful than a life spent doing nothing.

- ❖ Remember that you can't please everyone. Nobody can.

- ❖ Take a few minutes to listen to a motivational audio program to recharge your mind with positive thoughts.

- ❖ Talk to an encouraging and supportive friend.

- ❖ Sometimes you do need to let certain people go. This step can lighten your load, enabling you to focus on more positive interactions.

Staying Positive

There are four mental musts for maintaining a positive attitude and inspiring it in others: optimism, objectivity, deliberateness, and determination.

- ❖ **Optimism** is critical to building your business and achieving the better life you want. No matter what has happened in your past, the here and now is yours to build with, and the future is yours to influence. As Organic Principle #6—Persistence states, there is a connection between the effort you make today and the success you find tomorrow. Recently, I took a trip to Toronto, Canada. While there, I decided to visit the first home my mother and I stayed in when we arrived from Greece. I was surprised to discover that the old building is still being used for short-term housing for immigrants. I stood there and let the memories flow. In those early days, we received a government allowance of $200 a month, and out of that stipend we had to buy all of our groceries and clothing. It was a very tight budget! We managed to save every penny we could so that, once a week, we could afford a special dinner at my favorite fast-food restaurants. Imagine, two complete meals for less than $4.

Today, I realize how fortunate my mother and I were to have been selected to immigrate to Canada, as it literally changed my life and allowed me to flourish.

* **Objectivity** pushes you to be honest with everyone, especially with yourself. Admit when you mess up and give yourself credit for doing something well. Being honest boosts your self-esteem and contributes to building authentic, positive relationships.

  Objectivity is also necessary for making good decisions. When it comes to making good decisions, it isn't always necessary to present an opposing side, if you think an associate has a bad or unworkable idea. It's often better to let people work things out for themselves. If you feel responsible for the actions of other people, stop it! You can offer support to friends, but you can't live their lives for them.

* **Deliberateness** is the quality that empowers you to recognize behaviors that are holding you back. Once you are being honest with yourself, you will see some personal habits that you must make a conscious and conscientious effort to change. This follows Organic Principle #10—Discipline. Deliberateness means being thoughtful about your thinking and your actions. Once you recognize negative behavior, you can intentionally change it by replacing it with better habits.

* **Determination** connects with your drive. While being deliberate means being intentional about your thoughts and actions, being determined means being tough-minded about them. There is no point in giving up. Giving up makes you feel helpless. If you don't reach your goals on the first try, look for other ways to achieve them. While on a trip to Mexico, I met a gentleman who told me a very

moving story. About a year earlier, he had been caught in the crossfire of dispute and was shot six times. Three of the bullets came within an inch of his heart. His uncle was sprawled out on the pavement next to him with nine bullet wounds. Miraculously, they survived to tell their stories.

He told me, "Since the shooting, I am now one year old. I came to the realization that it was God's gift to me to have a second chance in life." He also shared that he had become an organic networker because it gave him the chance to help others and pay it forward with a selfless spirit.

Network marketing attracts people from all around the world who truly want to help others. Stories like this one demonstrate the positive, connective power of organic networking and why I love this profession!

SIDEBAR: GET CARDED

Presenting your business card is a great way to share information about you and your company. Some folks fear looking pushy or think handing out a business card is tacky. Let me dispel this myth. Giving out your business card lets people know who you are. In many parts of the world, particularly Asia, handing out your business card is actually a formal part of the introduction process. Keep your business cards with you at all times. You never know when you'll meet someone who can have a significant impact on your business!

Less Is More

Most of us derive tremendous pleasure from talking about ourselves. However, when someone uses every opportunity to wax on about this achievement or that problem, others eventually get tired of the egotistical attitude. When you are more willing to listen to others, friends and associates not only appreciate you more, they are also more open to what you have to say. Consider the advice of a Greek philosopher, Epictetus: Nature gave us one tongue and two ears so we could hear twice as much as we speak.

As a frequent public speaker, I must admit that I love to talk! But there are times when a person just wants me to listen. As I began examining my conversations with others, the results were obvious. I talked much more than I listened! However, over the years, a kind of inner radar has developed in me. I don't know how it developed or when it started. I just knew, intuitively, that I needed to pay attention to how much I talked and how well I listened.

In order to train myself to listen more effectively, I took a huge first step. I decided to shut up. I only asked questions relating to the other person's comments and refused to create distractions. Sometimes, I literally bit my tongue. A key insight about relationship-building soon became clear to me: People genuinely respond to active listening.

A business colleague and I used to share our perspectives on what it is like to network at events where we don't know a soul. Those conversations got me thinking about what works for me.

First, I make a point of not talking about my business or myself. Rather than volunteer information, I respond only when asked, even if I'm the one who initiated the conversation. This focus on the other person has helped me build trust and credibility with the types of people that I want to align myself with.

Second, although the initial conversation may focus on business, I always shift the subject to the other person's personal interests. There is no way to connect with someone in business without knowing something about their personal lives. Small chunks of information, like birthdays, hobbies, and names of family members can go a long way when used properly.

Let Go of Gossip

Once you make positive relationships a priority, you will never again take pleasure in commenting on someone's frequent failings. I also advise you to keep in mind a Spanish proverb: *Whoever gossips to you will gossip about you.* Subconsciously, no one really trusts people who gossip. This bad habit inevitably weakens relationships because it requires dwelling on negative aspects. Organic networkers are invested in a positive attitude and avoid gossip at all cost.

Check Your Motives

Genuine relationships are based on mutual support and goodwill, irrespective of any personal gain, real or hoped for. When you view a relationship from the perspective of what you can get out of a person, you soon discover that other people have a similar way of looking at you. Relationships based on selfish motives are also tentative ones and rarely positive in the truest sense.

My advice is to establish connections that are grounded in mutual benefit. Whether meeting face to face or communicating online, the goal is to provide helpful information or to assist with a new connection. Once trust is built, a return favor from the other person is usually inevitable and unsolicited.

The Power of Oneness

Relationship-building is based on a simple but essential premise: Treat others as you would like others to treat you. That means embracing and developing a feeling of oneness. You will find it difficult to say or do anything that could cause suffering or discomfort to anyone. Every time you open your mouth or decide to do something, you will always consider the impact of your words and actions on others.

Oneness also has a wonderful way of inspiring us to release any feelings of superiority and inferiority. Mike, a very good business friend of mine from Vancouver, Canada, has been a living testimony to the concept of oneness and Organic Principle #11— Respect for as long as I've known him. Not only is he an extremely giving person, he also gives without ever demanding a return favor. I've never seen him in conflict or showing disrespect to another human being. It should come as no surprise that I have also never heard a single complaint about him from anyone. His attitude and behavior are a perfect example of Organic Principle #8—Relationships.

Bring on the Humor

Another golden rule of mine is: Never take yourself too seriously. This doesn't mean that we welcome humiliation. Far from it. Having a sense of humor means that we let go of that voice in our heads that urges us to be judgmental and tells us that it's us versus them in business. Humor is a connective force and often the best antidote for relieving tense situations.

Many relationship problems could be avoided if a smile or more relaxed attitude was involved. My uncle once offered me the following insight:

- ❖ 80 percent of our worries have already happened.

- ❖ 10 percent of our worries might happen.

- ❖ 10 percent of our worries we have no control over.

This wisdom tells us to lighten up. It's always better to contribute toward a positive outcome, rather than allowing a problem or situation drag us down.

Putting Others First

You can build positive relationships regardless of the venue or situation. The same skills apply whether you are:

- At a social gathering or party

- Talking on the telephone

- Meeting new people for the first time

- Visiting the library or the museum

- At your place of work

- At meetings where you are promoting your network marketing business

- Social networking

With a single goal, you will interact with people from all walks of life—another positive relationship in your life. The means to achieving that end is the power of putting others first. It's always worth making any interaction one that brings a little light to the other person's day. When you adopt this approach, you will inevitably experience positive benefits in your own life, bringing a little light to your relationships at work, in the family, at church, everywhere!

Organic networking works best for me when I look for opportunities to do something kind for someone else. My method is pay it forward with a twist. Pay it forward is about connecting good deeds with other good deeds. You do something nice for someone and, in return, you ask only that they do the same for someone else. The organic networking approach takes pay it forward to the next level, where good deeds benefit both of you at the same time.

When I meet a new person at an event, I introduce myself and start a conversation. However, in the back of my mind I am asking myself, "Is there something I can do for this person?" Sure, the interaction may result in a sale or a new distributor, but I allow this kind of outcome to happen naturally. Because the other person and I have made a connection, based on Pay It Forward 2.0, we both benefit at the same time.

Breaking the Ice

If you have ever felt awkward with someone you have never met before, join the club! Shyness is a part of being human, especially when approaching new people for the first time. Self-doubt can race through our brains as we mentally scramble to find the perfect conversation starter. Trust me; it gets easier.

In the early phase of any relationship, it's natural to experience:

- A fluttering heart rate

- Sweaty palms

- Dry mouth

- General anxiety

- Stumbling over words

As you engage with the other person, a shift occurs. In this more comfortable phase, you feel:

- A slower, relaxed heart rate

- Drier palms

- No more dry mouth

- Feelings of ease

- A readiness to laugh

- A more natural flow to the conversation

It helps to keep in mind that there are no perfect opening lines to guarantee your success. There are, however, some simple guidelines to help you move past the early-phase jitters more quickly.

Put On Your Smile

Before you say a single word, put a smile on your face. A smile not only puts people you interact with, who are probably just as apprehensive as you are, at ease. It puts you in the right frame of mind. Smile when you communicate face-to-face and even when you are on the phone. Smile until your cheek muscles ache!

Be All Ears

As I mentioned earlier, learn to listen well. Your prospects and customers will want to do business with you. You'll keep distributors and develop lifelong friendships. You'll manage conflicts more effectively. You'll be more creative and connected. You'll grow as a leader, drawing people to you. It's a fact, by becoming a better listener, you'll be more influential in everything you do.

Be Completely Involved

I make it a point to be completely involved in everything I do and with everyone I meet. This means that 100 percent of my mind, body, and spirit is right there with the person in front of me. I stay focused on them, in that moment.

One of the basic truths about being completely involved is that there's no way anyone can fake it. How long does it take you to recognize when someone is not really there with you? If you are like me, I can tell, in a matter of moments, when someone is not with me over the phone.

Being completely involved is not a technique. It is a conscious choice we make by shifting our mindset with the following techniques:

- ❖ Let the other person be the star. By giving others the spotlight, we can recognize and help develop other leaders.

- ❖ Focus on what is being said. Don't plan what you will say next, while the other person is speaking.

- ❖ Let the other person finish. Don't start talking until the other person is done.

- ❖ Allow moments of silence. When the other person stops talking, let their words sink in, and then respond.

- ❖ Review the important points when you start speaking. Make sure you heard the other person correctly.

- ❖ Offer your feedback, sharing your thoughts and ideas on what you heard.

SIDEBAR: GET CLOSER

For the next 30 days, pick one person in your life with whom you can commit to be more present. That doesn't mean you have to spend more time with this person. When you're with him or her, stop what you are doing, turn off all your devices, and look at the person with fresh eyes and an open heart. Ask more questions, then stop and listen. I have found that as you experience a deeper connection with someone, you will become thirsty for more connections. Soon, being completely involved becomes a natural habit.

Asking Questions

Questions are essential to the conversation process, but it is crucial to recognize that there are two types of questions.

❖ **Closed questions** can be answered with a single word, yes/no, or a short phrase. These questions often begin with the words: do, would, are, will, or if. For example, if you were to ask, "Do you have any children?" You will probably get a single word or short response. Closed questions also keep control of the conversation with the questioner. I have found that closed questions are useful when beginning a conversation, as they are easy to answer and do not force the other person to reveal too much before they are ready. An opinion can also be framed as a closed question, simply by adding a tag, such as: isn't it?, don't you?, or can't they?

Some examples of closed questions:

❖ A home-based business is a terrific way to earn extra income, isn't it?

❖ Are you enjoying the seminar?

❖ San Diego's weather is amazing, isn't it?

❖ **Open questions** are designed to elicit a longer, more detailed answer. Although any question can trigger a long answer, open questions deliberately seek longer and more informative responses. The questions begin with words or phrases like: what, why, how, describe, or tell me. For example, if you were to ask, "What did you do over the holidays?" The response will come with some details attached, which will allow you to ask a follow-up question.

Some examples of open questions are:

❖ Tell me about your job.

❖ How did you decide to choose China for your vacation?

❖ What would this opportunity mean to you and your family?

❖ Open questions ask respondents to think and reflect, and open them up to sharing opinions and feelings. Using open questions can be uncomfortable, even scary, at first. They seem to take control of the conversation away from you, the questioner, and hand it over to the other person. However, well-placed open questions actually keep you in control. This is especially true as the respondent relaxes. That's the point where you can direct the conversation to wherever you want it to go.

Remember that positive relationships require building rapport, and open questions are your number one tool for this objective. When I start a conversation, the ratio that works for me is three closed questions to one open question. The closed questions make both of us feel more comfortable. The open question then gets the other person thinking and inevitably offering meaningful information.

Keep asking open questions until you find a connection point. Be patient. Nowhere is it written that bonding with another person has to happen quickly. It takes time to build a real relationship. It has been my experience that fostering a strong business relationship can take months, if not years. Don't abandon a potential relationship because it takes a while to build rapport.

ORGANICWISE:

Building relationships takes time, just as it takes time for a seed to grow into an apple tree. You cannot buy true friendship. It must be formed organically, one conversation or experience at a time, in order to last. Once you internalize this truth, organic relationships will be the only ones you'll have and enjoy.

Accentuate the Positive

Each day I know that I am blessed to have had the opportunity to experience some of the greatest gifts that life has to offer. Among those treasures is the gift of friendship. I am fortunate to have crossed paths with people around the world, learning about different cultures and unique perspectives. While great friendships may be rare in this world, positive connections with people are always available to you. Now you, too, have the tools you need to make that happen!

Chapter 7

THE 3 QS OF ORGANIC RECRUITING

I have been asked more times than I can count, "So, Kosta, just how do you decide which people to approach when it comes to building your network marketing business?" My answer, "It doesn't matter! You never know which prospect will pursue an organic networking opportunity with a vengeance."

Diamonds in the Rough

Ever wonder why a high-quality diamond is so expensive? I once watched a PBS documentary on mining for diamonds. Although there are four basic ways to mine diamonds, to find a one carat diamond that will make it to Tiffany & Co., in New York, whatever method of mining is being employed, you would have to mine 250 tons of dirt to find one perfect diamond. Do the math. For you to pan for and find one high quality diamond, you would have to sift through one ton of dirt every day for 250 days. If you prefer to hire employees and purchase the equipment necessary to mine diamonds, it will cost you an average of $6 million per year to stay in business.

There are two distinct classes of diamonds. One is of industrial quality and ends up attached to the ends of drill-bits, grinding away at honing medical devices and other industrial products. The other is polished and ends up as—you guessed it – the high quality diamond at Tiffany's.

When I agreed to go to my very first network marketing meeting, I was a university student who thought making an extra $1,000 a month sounded like a great idea. As I pulled up to the huge house where the meeting was being held, the long driveway was lined with gleaming luxury cars. I sheepishly parked my ancient Ford Escort on the street.

Once inside the home, I was introduced to four men wearing suits that were worth more than my car. As I entered the meeting room dressed in faded jeans, sandals, an earring, wild t-shirt, and long hair, I was definitely an industrial-quality diamond. My heart was pounding in my chest, but I acted as cool and confident as possible under the circumstances. I thought to myself: These people have money. Could I be successful like them?

I immediately understood that it was time to draw a line in the sand, zip my lip, listen, and become a young CANEI sponge. I listened intently for hours. Finally, it was after midnight, and the only people left were the meeting host and me. I was hooked! The host told me that if I wanted what he had, he would help me build a business, just like someone had helped him when he first started.

With no experience whatsoever, I signed up with the dream of making millions. I maxed out my credit card and borrowed money from family and friends to pay the enrollment fee. The products were delivered to my house about a week later. Within 30 days,

I had quit school and my job and was ready to make it big. The top leaders were doing well, right? Full of energy and enthusiasm, I started recruiting, and to me that meant recruiting any human being around me whom I could find breathing.

It looked good at first. My first month's check was $2,800, and I was sure I'd be a millionaire in 12 months. Every night, I took new recruits to a meeting, loading up my car with as many people as it would hold. Within 90 days, I had signed up 96 distributors. But, when it came time for my distributors to renew their annual membership for a second year, the only people remaining in my downline were my mother, my aunt, my uncle, and my sister. I paid their memberships.

What could have gone wrong? Why had all of the distributors I'd worked so hard to recruit and train just faded away? These were such important questions. Looking back, I wish that I could have had a blueprint for success, like Organic Networker, to follow during those early days.

I struggled with my early failures until I eventually realized that there are three different qualities of diamonds in network marketing—what I call the 3 Qs:

1. Quantity Prospects

2. Quality Prospects

3. Qualified Prospects

Once I was able to differentiate these three groups, I was able to better focus my efforts.

	QUANTITY	**QUALITY**	**QUALIFIED**
Education	High School	Some College or University	High School or above
Current Occupation	Various	Manager Professional or Executive	Network Marketer
Current Income Level	Low to Middle 5 Figures	High 5 Figures to Low 6 Figures	Variable
Income Expectations	Middle to High 5 figures	Middle 6 Figures to 7 Figures	Middle 6 Figures to 7 Figures
Turnover Rate	High	Medium	Medium to High
Maintenance Level	High	Low	Medium to High
Motivation	Income-Recognition	Recognition-Income	Income-Recognition

❖ **The Quantity Group.** The Quantity group is a massive target market. These prospects typically fall into the lower- to middle-income bracket, own a small business, work in a service industry, or have a blue-collar job. A large group like this is always alluring to a new organic networker. In fact, this is the group of prospects I focused on when I first started. I was like a tornado that tore through everyone in my path – from my family, to the mailman, to the barista in the coffee shop.

These individuals are recruited the fastest of the 3 Qs. This group wants to supplement their income and, given the proper motivation and leadership, may eventually replace it. Because they are new to network marketing, they have a higher learning curve and require considerable support to get started. Their level of turnover will also be the highest of the 3 Qs, especially if they do not make money within the first 90 days. In line with Organic Principle #10— Leadership, you will need to provide the in-the-trenches training and encouragement needed to keep them moving forward.

ORGANICWISE:

In general, the best way to guarantee success at recruiting is to follow the system the company has put in place. However, recruitment is a process that needs to be done organically to reap the greatest results. The organic system of recruitment means having a clear understanding of the 3 Qs and what will motivate members of each group to join your company.

* **The Quality Group.** The Quality group is composed of individuals we would call, accomplished business people. The group members have achieved some level of success in their chosen fields or industries, either working for a company as a senior manager or self-employed and running their own business. Quality group members demand the best and are willing to pay for it. They usually do more due-diligence before buying into your company. While some people feel this group is tougher to recruit, as an organic networker I will tell you that they are not.

Quality prospects can see the potential of network marketing, but they may not yet have the burning financial need to build a business. Organic Principle #7—Patience is important because, if you are patient with Quality prospects and take the time needed to get them to identify their personal, why, the payoff is usually good. They are attuned to the organic process of setting goals and work methodically to achieve them, as they know that it takes time to build a business. Once they've made a commitment, they will leverage their professional credibility to solicit and attract high-quality prospects. An added plus is that they are already comfortable expecting to earn a seven-figure income.

This group is generally motivated by recognition and a sense of being important to the organization. Over the years, I have personally witnessed many millionaires join this profession for one important and organic reason: They wanted to be recognized as an important part of something larger than themselves. I know a couple who had made their fortune in real estate before getting involved in my company. In fact, they had retired and planned on traveling around the world on their hundred-foot yacht. Ultimately, they were more excited about getting on the stage and being recognized for their efforts, than they were about the handsome bonus they were collecting.

❖ **The Qualified Group.** The Qualified group includes seasoned, professional network marketers. These people have built a team in the past, are currently building a team, or believe it or not, may be looking for a new venture. They thrive on the organic process of building a business from the ground up. Of course, these experienced networkers usually bring with them an enormous group of followers from their former or existing venture.

The turnover rate of this group is quite high, and their departure can generate great disappointment in the company they leave behind. The good news is that once Qualified individuals are locked in to your business, the only thing you need to do is to get out of their way and let them grow and expand their business. These powerhouses have the ability to grow a business tenfold in a very short period of time. Their passion for the organic process to success can also create enormous momentum across the organization.

Considered the high producers, Qualified prospects will demand much more personal recognition and business perks than the other two groups. Their requests will run the gamut, from wining-and-dining to additional on-going bonuses, up to and including major recognition incentives.

While you will find and develop leaders from each of the 3 Qs, most often the finest diamonds are mined from the Qualified group. What you want to keep an eye out for are the Qualified prospects. I call them, REAL (Realistic Experienced Aggressive Leaders). You can identify leaders that are REAL by asking the following questions and measuring their answers against the guidelines provided.

* How long have they been in the industry? A minimum of five years and an average of fifteen years is the standard.

* How many network marketing companies have they represented? Anything more than three companies over a decade is too many.

* How large is the group they have built in their most recent company? This one depends on the type of compensation plan. In a usual Breakaway or Uni-level, the ratio is 1:10 as compared to Binary. So, if a Breakaway or Uni-level leader has a decent-sized group of a few thousand active distributors, an equivalent Binary leader should have 20,000 to 30,000 distributors in their group.

* What are their financial accomplishments? An average income for a leader in this profession is $10,000 a month. Anything less is considered, leader-in-making. Remember, the key to financial success comes from long-term commitment, not short-term hits. This means you measure what they average over a twelve-month period and not their biggest paycheck.

* How long ago did they achieve those numbers? I always suggest that you look no further than the last three years, unless someone has left the profession within those years. Note: Leaders in the Binary world should be expected to show much greater financial achievement than other comp plan producers. Once again, $10,000 a month in Uni-level is equivalent to $20,000 to $30,000 a month in Binary.

❖ What is their ability to duplicate and replicate their successful leadership style? This involves Organic Principle #10—Leadership and includes the following:

  ❖ Their system in place for duplication

  ❖ Their relationship with their top leaders

  ❖ Their fan base within their downline

Quick-to-Leap

Now that you are familiar with the 3 Qs, let's close this chapter by identifying a less-appealing group that could have a detrimental impact on your business. These individuals are what I refer to as, the Serial Network Marketers. In the Q-world, we would describe them as, Quick-to-Leap!

These network marketers take great pride in joining any new company they see as more exciting than their present or old company. They typically jump ship to the next greatest company in the world after just a few short months. Will they build in your business? Not likely. Will they attract other distributors to your business? Yes, but beware. They will attract other serial network marketers. Will they become a good referral for you? No, because their reputation for being quick leapers and their subsequent lack of credibility in the profession could potentially do much more damage to your organization than the short-term volume they might produce.

Quick-to-Leap distributors are looking for the easy pot of gold at the end of the next rainbow. They take great pride in their association with many companies and have loyalty to none. Few members of this group ever achieve a reasonable level of financial success. You would be well advised to avoid recruiting them.

The key to successful recruiting is to build your business with a good mix of Quantity, Quality, and Qualified members. While there are exceptions to any rule, about 99 percent of all of your prospective recruits fall into one of these Q-categories.

By adhering to Organic Principle #11—Respect and recognizing the strengths, weaknesses, and motivations for all three Q-groups, you'll know what to expect from them and what they will expect from you. With the right blend of positive, motivated Quantity, Quality, and Qualified distributors, you will be rewarded with a productive blend of team members dedicated to the organic process and driven to succeed.

Chapter 8

GIVING PRAISE AND CRITICISM

As an organic networker, giving and receiving praise and criticism can become a normal part of building your team. Good news or praise is always easy to give and receive because it delivers positive feelings. On the other hand, bad news or criticism causes emotions no one wants to feel. Bad news, however, can actually be good news, depending upon the attitude of the giver and the receiver.

A good leader will always find a way to turn a negative situation into a positive one.

Leading a Volunteer Army

One of the most formidable and brilliant leaders in history, Attila the Hun, was the subject of a book written by Wess Roberts, Ph.D., titled, *Leadership Secrets of Attila the Hun*. Attila was twelve years old when his father died, and he was held hostage in the hated Roman court of Honorius. Attila decided to study his enemy's culture and their political, military, and leadership strategies, which he used to build an army to conquer the world.

Attila was a brilliant leader who led a horde of seven hundred thousand men who were a confederation of fiercely independent multiracial and multilingual tribes. They had no observable religion or form of government. Attila had no way to pay his fighting forces except with the booty of victory.

Attila's dilemma was the same dilemma that network marketing leaders face today, which is to decide on the leadership method to use so that their distributors will voluntarily follow them.

Given this premise, Attila formulated his leadership style organically, from the ground up. He developed a set of principles that would allow potential leaders, given their commitment, to mature into leadership roles. He did not believe that by simply becoming the best archer or swordsman or the bravest man on the battlefield qualified anyone to be a leader. These were certainly admirable characteristics, but they were not what Attila was looking for in a leader. His principles, according to Roberts, were loyalty, courage, desire, emotional and physical stamina, empathy, decisiveness, anticipation, timing, competitiveness, self-confidence, accountability, responsibility, credibility, tenacity, dependability, and stewardship, which meant that subordinates were not to be abused but developed and rewarded for their performance.

Understanding that leadership was to be earned, Attila said, "Those of you who are overly ambitious may attempt to acquire these qualities over a short period. As I, Attila, have found in my own life, these qualities of leadership simply take time, learning and experience to develop. There are few who will find shortcuts. There are simply rare opportunities to accelerate competence, and without paying the price, no matter how great or small, none will become prepared to lead others. Learn these leadership skills well. Teach them to the Huns. Only then will we expand our ability to lead our vast nation in pursuit of world conquest."

Attila believed that once you developed into a leader, to attract and train other potential leaders, the leader was required to have resilience to overcome personal misfortune, discouragement, rejection and disappointment...You must be willing to make unrecognized and thankless and personal sacrifice for those you serve and those you lead.

Without a doubt, if Attila was building a network marketing business, today, and applied his leadership principles, he would be a prime example of an organic networker. Like Attila, as in organic networking, you don't hire and oversee people as you would in a traditional business. Distributors are not paid a salary, and you are not their boss. They do not punch a time clock or risk being fired because they didn't put in enough time or commitment. Therefore, an effective leader must develop the skills required to lead by example and to influence a volunteer army of distributors.

Another distinction between a traditional business and network marketing is that unhappy employees can look for a job with another company. In network marketing, dissatisfied members on your team simply quit working. However, many remain in the company, rather than resign, and they become deadweight distributors and drag down the momentum of your team. In line with Organic Principle #10—Leadership, it is your responsibility to create an environment that encourages team members to grow, personally and professionally.

One of my leadership skills is my ability to create and foster, as Attila did, the feeling of belonging to something bigger than any single individual. If you lead by example, people will line up to join your volunteer army.

The Value of Praise

It is widely accepted that everyone, employees and distributors alike, consistently rank appreciation for work well done high on the motivation index. In fact, one of the reasons distributors disengage from a company is the lack of praise and recognition.

Commit to the following leadership strategies:

- Value: Give distributors a sense of importance about who they are and how you value their role in the organization.

- Connection: Make sure that distributors know that company leaders genuinely care about them. Distributors have to feel a connection with their leaders.

- Gratitude: Let your people know that they are appreciated for their contributions and sacrifices.

- Fairness: Ensure that your distributors recognize that you are dedicated to an equal and fair distribution of rewards.

Recognition and praise are high octane fuel for the soul. They also inspire an individual to go the extra mile for the person who offered the compliment. If this wasn't true, none of us would bother keeping and savoring all of the awards, plaques, trophies, congratulatory notes, and *atta-boy* emails we've received over the years.

Intuitively, we know that genuine appreciation is necessary in our relationships with team members and fellow distributors. Yet many well-meaning and otherwise caring leaders are reluctant to praise the talents and contributions of others.

Many years ago, I worked for a great boss, Roy, who confided in me that he found offering praise a very difficult thing to do, both publicly and, even harder, privately. I asked him why that was, and he said, "I grew up in a household where praising others was not something we did." Roy's answer hit me like a ton of bricks! Behaviors learned early in life can be difficult to break as we move through adulthood.

When we withhold praise, we are limiting our ability to connect with people. Organic networkers need to get past any long-held reluctance, embarrassment, or shyness. Besides improved connections, there is another benefit, as the Chinese saying goes, "A bit of perfume always clings to the hand that gives roses." Giving praise also makes the giver feel good.

Some pointers for overcoming roadblocks to expressing appreciation:

❖ Find the Root Cause of Your Fear. If you have difficulty giving praise, discover and analyze the root causes of your resistance. For example, if it is a fear of embarrassing others, know that even the most introverted individuals, those who hate any kind of public attention, will enjoy reading an email applauding their contributions.

❖ Take the Time. Sometimes withholding praise is due to a lack of time. This is especially true when you are required to handle an ever-increasing number of issues during the course of an unreasonably busy day. If this is your challenge, I encourage you to rethink how you view the issue of giving praise. It takes less than ten seconds to say, "I appreciate the time and thought you put into organizing this meeting. It was exceptional. Thank you."

❖ Sooner than Later. Praise has a limited use-by date. Don't put it off for later or wait until the next time you see that individual. If you notice something worthy of praise, express your appreciation promptly.

❖ Be Specific. Make your words memorable by being specific about the achievement. Not many of us treasure that overused statement: Job well done! However, we all remember someone who tells us: This (fill in the blank) was pure genius. Or, I would have missed this (specify the detail), if you hadn't picked up on it.

ORGANICWISE:

The key to offering criticism and praise is to make sure that your words are genuine and grounded, as in Organic Principle #12—Humility. We each have our strengths and weaknesses. Treat the recipient of your comments with respect. Praise does not have to be elaborate, and neither does criticism. Simply be real and specific.

Connect Praise to the Big Picture.

The ultimate form of giving praise is letting people know that their specific work makes a difference to the entire organization. It doesn't matter how far removed a person is from the top of the organization. I believe in making everyone feel like an owner. My goal is to help each person understand how his or her work contributes to the big picture. Consistently develop the practice of noticing people's contributions. Excellence involves everyone!

Communicating Organic Criticism

Let's face it, very few people like criticism. The word, criticism, is possibly the most feared word when it comes to interaction between two people. Thousands of people have spent sleepless nights when their boss or manager, in no uncertain terms, told them that he wants to see them first thing in the morning. I must admit that, a few years ago, I was one of those people who felt very uncomfortable giving or receiving criticism, that is, until I learned that there are rules to organic criticism.

What Is Organic Criticism?

Organic criticism is one of the most important tools in your organic networking toolbox. It is accepted by mutual consent between two people, or among a group of people, with one sole purpose in mind: to achieve success.

The Three-Step Organic Criticism Formula

Step 1—Praise + Step 2—Constructive Criticism + Step 3—Praise = Improved Performance

As previously discussed, it takes an enormous amount of work to find, cut, and polish one high-quality diamond before it is placed into a showcase at Tiffany & Co., in New York. If a diamond cutter makes one tiny mistake, it could take the diamond from being priceless to being relegated to a wedding shop in Las Vegas. How you conform to the rule of organic criticism will help you find your diamond-in-the-rough and shape it into a shining superstar in the industry.

Soon after arriving in Canada, I took a job at a computer company and, one day, when my manager asked to talk to me, my stress immediately spiked, as I knew he was going to criticize my performance. But, as fate would have it, it was a meeting that, over time, led to the development of my approach to accepting and delivering criticism. Before starting the conversation, my manager made certain that no one was within earshot of our discussion. First, he complimented me on the tasks I was doing well. Second, he followed this with a gentle but specific set of criticisms broken down into short-term, achievable goals that addressed my weaknesses or where I needed improvement. Third, he gave me a gentle pat on the back, telling me that if I coupled his criticism with my enthusiasm and strengths, I would continue to improve and excel in my career.

The process was so smooth that I never felt threatened, and my initial fear of criticism disappeared. As he predicted, I did improve by leaps and bounds. The Three-Step Organic Criticism Formula is invaluable when it comes to building your organization. If you are one of those people who fear criticism, you can quit worrying.

Think of my formula as a delicious Subway sandwich. The top half of the bun represents the praise. The delicious ingredients represent the criticism and bite-size, achievable goals that are easy to swallow and digest. The bottom half of the bun represents the praise and pat on the back.

The positive benefits of using the organic criticism formula are fourfold:

- ❖ It naturally lowers defenses.

- ❖ You make the person feel appreciated.

- ❖ Positive feedback always garners positive results.

- ❖ The recipient will take your criticism and turn it into positive action.

How Criticism Fits into Your Organic Blueprint for Success

In organic networking, leaders are usually the ones delivering criticism, but they can also be the recipients. Problems arise when a leader fails to teach his or her team members the organic criticism formula. My suggestion is that you work with your team to make this formula flow seamlessly throughout your organization.

I am going to assume that you joined your company to achieve the lifestyle of your dreams. In that case, you must make it clear to every leader in your organization that you have a set of expectations that will be measured against their *Organic Blueprint for Success.*

Organic Principle #9—Wisdom features CANEI, which has one irrefutable basic principle: *The responsibility to improve your life is yours and yours alone.*

Most people who join network marketing companies are generally very rough diamonds that need to be patiently polished into high-quality, sparkling diamonds. They usually come from a highly structured employment environment. They must be at work by a certain time, have a job description to fulfill, take lunch at a certain hour, and report to a boss or manager, and initiative isn't always looked upon as a positive trait. A great number of these people will be new to network marketing. Others will have failed at one or more attempts at network marketing or made part-time income but could not break into the big leagues. Of course, you will attract experienced network marketers, but unless you are already highly successful, your chances of them joining your team will be few and far between.

When you sponsor prospects who come from highly structured employment backgrounds and ask them to design an *Organic Blueprint for Success*, take the initiative to write goals and the activities to fulfill those goals, and then carry out the plan without supervision, it is a recipe for disaster. It is important for you to take the initiative to give your leaders-in-training the opportunity to succeed. Discussing why and how leaders in network marketing should communicate criticism may seem out of place, since there is no boss or supervisor, employees, job descriptions, defined work schedule, guaranteed income or salaries, guaranteed benefits, and they can quit at the first obstacle.

Unfortunately, I have seen people, who possess high quality leadership skills, fade away because they fell short of becoming an organic network marketer. They helped their new diamond or prospect write goals and activities and offered a great deal of support but failed to criticize their nonperformance. In all the years that I have been in this industry, the one thing that drives me to distraction is a culture that says not to criticize or hold distributors accountable because you might hurt their feelings and they'll quit. If you are not willing to offer criticism, you will deprive yourself and your leaders-in-training the opportunity to succeed.

As an organic networker, you must draw a line in the sand and build your organization from the ground up, and you must teach your organization to do the same.

The Organic Criticism Formula Is Profitable

Remember:

* Schedule a weekly meeting, via phone, Skype, or in person to review and evaluate whether or not the agreed-upon organic blueprint activities, such as making 10 prospecting calls per day, have been met. Start every meeting with praise for the activities your leaders-in-training have done well.

* If there are activities that haven't been accomplished, you need to address each activity and why it wasn't accomplished. Was it because of a busy work schedule, watching too much TV, fear of rejection, or lack of focus or organizational skills?

* Whatever the reason for non-productiveness, you must find a solution as quickly as possible. If productivity is not evident over a couple of weeks, find out whether your leaders really believe in their goals and are willing to draw a line in the sand and defy anyone or anything trying to stop them. If they are not willing to do this, it is best that you cut your losses and move on.

* It is important that you play an active role in defining and resolving the solution. If your leaders-in-training have call-reluctance or fear of rejection, you may want to spend

several evenings role-playing, making a few calls for them as a learning tool, or doing three-way prospecting calls.

❖ If the solution is to change behavior, you must define the behavior. If your leaders can't miss their favorite prime-time TV program, the solution may be to record the program and watch it at a later time or turn the TV off. For every behavior that needs to be addressed, offer solutions that will push the problem behavior to the background and the corrective behavior to the forefront.

❖ Always give your leaders a pat on the back for their strengths, and help them outline what must be done to improve their weaknesses. Keep in mind that if someone has received this type of feedback at their job, it was usually negative and ego-diminishing.

❖ You will be amazed at the relationships you will build when your leaders realize that your praise and criticism helps them move closer to achieving their dreams and enriching their lives.

❖ Your role is to work with them to change their behavior and then applaud their improvements. The better they feel about themselves, the harder they will work to improve, personally and professionally.

❖ By the end of your meeting with them, always give your leaders-in-training measurable tasks to achieve for the following week, and let them know how much you value working with them.

In my opinion, there are two types of criticism: (1) The criticism that is addressed in hundreds of books and workshops that generally focus on how to tear someone down and then build them back up, or (2) Kosta's Organic Criticism Formula that focuses on one thing and one thing only: achieving goals set by your leader and not by you, helping them define their weaknesses and turn them into strengths by mutual consent, and patting them on the back for the tasks done well. Therefore, your leaders will become their own best critics and will have no excuse for nonperformance because they will have defined, with your input, exactly what they must do to reach their goals.

Understand that it takes an enormous amount of work to polish your diamonds, once you have found them, and you and your diamonds must take responsibility for the outcome. The formula works like this: Your leaders-in-training must draw a line in the sand and defy anyone or anything to try to stop them; write goals, activities, and work effort to achieve their dreams, in which the leader plays an active role.

If you find two very rough diamonds per year and polish them into high-quality diamonds, they will be worth a thousand times more than a room full of industrial diamonds that continue to grind away at a mediocre job, no matter how much you try to guide them down an alternative path.

Chapter 9

ORGANIC PARTNERSHIPS IN NETWORK MARKETING

Organic partnerships in network marketing usually involve the people closest to you. That makes it one of the more sensitive topics to write about. If you live in a typical family situation, both adults probably work, bustling each morning to get your children off to school or daycare. After work, there's cooking, cleaning, and homework until bedtime. As parents, you might get a couple of hours of free time before you hit the sack. The next morning, you get up and do it all over again. Balancing business with family life is challenging for most of us. It can be even more difficult when you and your spouse or significant other run a home-based business.

When the business is organic networking, the pluses can far outweigh the minuses. You and your partner set your own hours, co-manage the company, and work from home. You can also have more time to spend with the people most important to you. Minuses include the sacrifice of personal time. Movie nights go on the back burner and vacations get postponed.

Because organic networking doesn't follow the one-size-fits-all, traditional business model, it demands more of your attention in the early development stages than a traditional company or small business. Add to this the fact that many organic networkers start their business while still working a full-time job or raising children. Their network marketing opportunity is a second business, literally and figuratively.

Building Together

I have witnessed many families launch an organic networking business, successfully merging their work life and their home life. It has also been my experience that if the family suffers, the business suffers, and vice versa. For most of us, it can be difficult to create a separation between the demands of our work and the needs of our loved ones. Finding the right life-work balance is, therefore, essential to running a business from home.

How do you find that balance? You set up an organized, sustainable organic networking business from the get-go. It starts with Organic Principle #1—Readiness, which is a major asset when it comes to avoiding any future long-term problems.

A network marketing partnership will follow many of the standard procedures used by other entrepreneurial startups. This includes developing a business plan. It doesn't matter whether you're working with a family member, a friend, or a business associate, you need a business plan that clearly defines relevant information, such as:

- ❖ The concept of your business

- ❖ How much money you'll need for start-up costs

- ❖ Where and how the business will fit into the current market

- ❖ What kind of return on investment should be expected

As with any business, it's extremely important to understand what your goals are before you start building for the long term. Goals will be easier to measure once you create a vision for your company and understand both the short- and long-term milestones. Partners, couples, and family members should dedicate time to finding the personal, why, behind this question:

Why are you getting involved in a home-based network marketing business?

Once you know what you collectively want out of this business, it will be easier to focus on taking the steps needed to become successful organic networkers.

Define Your Roles

Conflict can rear its ugly head when partners make incorrect assumptions about who's responsible for what regarding business tasks. Get in front of this issue by holding a strategy meeting where you list the daily, weekly, and monthly tasks that are required for the family business. Some of the points to be discussed could include:

- ❖ Who designs or manages the website?

- ❖ Who deals with the social-networking sites and emails?

- ❖ Who makes sales calls?

- ❖ Who follows up with clients?

- ❖ Who conducts the meetings?

- ❖ Who prepares for the meetings?

- ❖ Who purchases products and supplies?

- ❖ Who writes the checks?

- ❖ Who deals with the existing members?

- ❖ How will we delegate the household chores?

Working together, delegate someone for each task, and post the list so that each person knows what is expected of him or her. In line with Organic Principle #3—Organization, all members of a family business should have clearly defined roles from the beginning. Avoid vague responsibilities, as they lead to confusion, and confusion leads to conflict. To avoid this, someone should be put in charge of the business, and the rest of the family should agree to respect that person's authority. If you opt to leave big decisions up to the family or group as a whole, come up with a specific plan for managing disagreements.

Respect Each Other's Talents

A successful partnership means having a collective understanding of how to best utilize each other's talents and leverage each other's strengths. Unfortunately, this is the part of the plan where couples and family members often take each other for granted. Organic Principle #8—Relationships, and Organic Principle #11—Respect become invaluable here!

I often tell family members and partners how fortunate they are to work together in an organic networking business. They have the opportunity to double or triple their efforts and grow the business much faster and larger than one individual could. Some of these partnerships followed the guidelines in this chapter to a T. They began by setting up the basic parameters and delegating tasks in a way that respectfully takes into account each person's strengths and weaknesses. They also excel at creating a mini-system within the family to balance their personal and business lives. This groundwork then expanded easily, as the business grew.

One couple I know has just about mastered these concepts. They conduct a mini board meeting for their family every Sunday, where they review plans for the upcoming week and check their short- and long-term goals. These meetings have motivated the children to contribute more. They can see how much work is involved in running a network marketing business, making them appreciate the rewards on a deeper level than their peers.

I was pleased to watch as this couple became millionaires after a few years of focused effort. They benefited along the way by leveraging their individual strengths and balancing their personal lives and the demands of the business.

SIDEBAR: POST IT

Post a whiteboard listing the tasks that each person is responsible for on a daily basis. Even if the To-Dos repeat every day, the wall chart will keep everyone clear on who's doing what. It can also help forecast when your spouse or partner might have an extra-heavy workload. Then you can take on some extra tasks to help out.

Spell Out Investor Rights

If someone from the family, either inside or outside the business, contributes financially, the terms of that contribution need to be put in writing. If your parents give you a startup loan, for example, write out the terms of how the loan is to be repaid, including interest terms. If the contribution is an investment, write out what the investment includes (part-ownership, dividends, voting rights, etc.). I recommend having an attorney draw up the papers, especially if the money loaned is a significant amount.

Protect Family Members

Family businesses can be operated as a legal entity in a variety of ways. Selecting the best legal entity can protect you and your family members from personal liability, if the business doesn't do well. If you don't know how to establish your business, get the advice of an attorney and an accountant specializing in home-based businesses.

Resolving Conflict

Eventually, you and your business partner are going to have a fight about the business. It's inevitable, and you need to work it out. The issue is usually a communication breakdown. When this happens, get out of the house and have a meeting in a neutral territory, such as a coffee shop or other public place, where you have to keep your voices down.

As you start to discuss the issue, do not get into finger-pointing. Do your best to figure out what happened and how to prevent it from happening again. Forgive each other; lay out the expectations, and move on. Remember, personal relationships and family connections come first. Agree, ahead of time, to keep any personal problems out of the business as much as possible.

I remember a particular couple who had issues in business and at home, including many conflicts that had never been resolved. Their children were not involved in the business and were obviously unhappy with their parents' choice to run a home-based company. The negativity of this couple affected other couples within their team, spreading like a virus.

Running a business creates enough drama; you don't need to add to it with family conflicts. It's crucial that you set up a system to facilitate communication, avoid miscommunication, and repair relationship connections when anger flares up.

ORGANICWISE:

As we learned, a genuine partnership grows organically from the first meeting to marriage. Joined by common goals, partners align their talents and patiently build the business, brick by brick. The force of two creates a doubled effect and provides a strong foundation for steady growth.

Getting Children Involved

Running a family business can be very tiring and frustrating for your children, especially in the early days when you're getting everything up and running. Children may start to miss Mom and Dad during this period. Involving them in the business, and doing this early on, is a powerful and easy way to spend more time with them and help them appreciate what you're doing. The couple I shared about earlier is a prime example of this.

Think of ways to hire your children to work for the business. Even small children can fold flyers or perform simple clerical tasks. Older kids can learn bookkeeping and other tasks. Be sure to pay them for the work they do. If it's all work and no reward, children can grow up resenting the idea of a family business.

One of the best ways to train your children comes from Organic Principle #10—Leadership. Lead by example. It's about showing your children how to run a home-based business, rather than telling them. This is very similar to training a new distributor, with a minor difference in age. What I always suggest is to have your children around, age permitting, when you make calls or attend meetings, so they can see, hear, and learn firsthand.

I've seen many children in the profession become major players in their parents' businesses, simply by sharing the products or services with their friends at schools. One distributor couple I know have a daughter who attended public school with a child whose single mother was from Hong Kong. To make a long story short, the daughter shared the product with her friend, and fourteen months later the single mother was the Number 1 producer in that company, and the first couple to become instant millionaires.

SIDEBAR: TO SINGLE PARENTS

Single parents usually have to work twice as hard to accomplish what a couple can do. But I have also noticed a single-parent advantage in this profession. Kids in a single-parent household are usually more supportive of their mother or father, and if trained and guided well, they will contribute more to the family business than children in a traditional family.

Being a single parent in organic networking will require a lot of patience on the parent's part, but the rewards can be bigger, beginning with the higher level of motivational energy than found in traditional households.

Time to Play

All work and no play, as the saying goes! Be sure to establish some rewards for accomplishing your goals each week. Make sure those rewards involve getting everyone out of the house together. Do something fun for a couple of hours, and make a rule that no one will talk about business during family playtime.

Get Upline Support

When it comes to making tough decisions, everyone in this profession needs a mentor. A second opinion from a trusted associate outside of the family or partnership makes good business sense. Often, this resource is the upline person who brought you into the business. He or she can be a savvy and impartial resource. In order for your mentor to guide you well, you must share the honest and unbiased version of your story.

During my first couple of years as an organic networker, I consulted with my mentor on a weekly basis regarding professional challenges I was facing. I also went to him with family dilemmas that I experienced from time to time. The trust I had for my mentor allowed me to listen to his personal experiences and learn how others dealt with similar issues. I was basically learning from others' mistakes in order to avoid future pitfalls—Organic Principle #9—Wisdom, in action.

Prepare and Prosper

A husband-wife team that I knew, the guy was one of my mentors when I started out, became the ideal business partners that everyone talked about. From the beginning, they divided tasks between them, based on their core strengths, and made work fun and productive. Their pleasure escalated when they included their daughters in weekly activities.

Whenever I saw them at events I was fascinated by how well the family communicated with each other and how flawlessly they all worked together. Their connection on the stage and with other people was magical. That dynamic partnership doesn't come overnight. I was fortunate enough to watch them grow into that kind of relationship organically, over time. Whenever I showed up to their home, I could feel the good vibes and positivity. It made me feel great, so much so that I visited them as often as I could. I modeled my home life after what this couple had built. Because of my decision, the same positive partnership model duplicated itself throughout my team. This allowed me to have one of the greatest teams of happy couples in the company.

The intensity that comes with combining an entrepreneurial lifestyle with family relationships doesn't work for every couple. However, with the right intentions and preparation, you too can discover the independence and the rewards that come with working and playing together with a trusted partner or your family.

SECTION THREE

BUILDING YOUR BUSINESS

The consistency factor goes a long way when it comes to building and unifying a team. After all, that's what makes organic networking such a dynamic opportunity. You build a team, and then go above and beyond to help them succeed. That leads to lifetime residuals.

Chapter 10

BUILD LOCAL, THINK GLOBAL

When I first started, my two primary goals were financial freedom and entrepreneurship. Every day was about making it happen so that the money could start rolling in. Did I spend huge chunks of time in pursuit of my goals? Absolutely. Did I build a big business? Going from ninety-six distributors to only four loving, but reluctant family members in one year was not what I had in mind! What I was missing in my process were the rules of the road for building a business. I had no blueprint to follow.

Of course, when I was in my early twenties, the last thing I was looking for was a set of rules. But with time and experience comes wisdom. Consider one of my favorite quotes from famous British World War II pilot Douglas Bader, "Rules are for the obedience of fools and the guidance of wise men." Some tried-and-true guidelines from the experts would have served me well when I started building my business.

The rules in this chapter are not to be followed blindly. Think of them as invaluable tools for crafting and shaping a business in a way that is easy to duplicate. That's what makes these rules organic. If you follow my guidelines, a recruit will realize what has worked for you, incorporate the same toolbox, and conclude: I see how he did it. If he can do it, so can I.

ORGANICWISE:

A system that is easy to duplicate is organic. Wherever you plant it, it will grow and spread. If a prospect doubts his or her ability to replicate your business and its systems, the chances of getting that person to sign up with you are slim to none. To paraphrase an old saying: *If you think you can't, you won't, no matter how big the carrot appears to be.* Your job is to have a replicable system in place that dissolves any doubts. Your prospect has to believe that he or she can easily apply your system to their own business.

Mr. K's Rules

Organic Principle #9—Wisdom tells us that when there's a chance to learn from the lessons of others and apply that knowledge to our business model, we leap at that opportunity. The wisdom I applied, as I built all of my successful businesses, utilizes a recruitment and expansion system that I call, Mr. K's Rules.

- ❖ **Recruit within Your Zip Code**
  Your Daily Motto: Sponsor Locally, Search Nationally. When your monthly earnings are less than $1,000 per month, sponsor and support new distributors that live near you. This area is best defined as your zip code or postal code region.

- ❖ **Recruit within Your Area Code**
  Your Daily Motto: Sponsor Locally, Search Globally. When your monthly earnings have increased to over $1,000

per month, but are still under $5,000 per month, sponsor and support distributors that live within your telephone area code.

- ❖ **Recruit within Your Country**
  Your Daily Motto: Support Locally, Sponsor Globally. Once your monthly earnings consistently exceed $5,000 per month, but fall under $10,000 per month, go ahead and sponsor new distributors and support existing distributors on a national basis.

- ❖ **Recruit within Your Continent**
  Your Daily Motto: Build Globally, Support Locally. When your monthly earnings are beyond $10,000 per month, but not yet consistently over $25,000 per month, expand your focus to recruits and distributors who live on the same continent as you.

- ❖ **Recruit Worldwide**
  Your Daily Motto: Build Globally, Support Globally. When your monthly earnings are over $100,000 per month, you can now build your business anywhere in the world.

SIDEBAR: MLM + MVM

While you are building your team of network marketing distributors using Mr. K's Rules, you can also make connections through multiviral marketing (MVM). This is done by carefully and strategically using social media sites, where you can reach and cater to a broader range of audiences around the world and from any device. MVM enables you to quickly and efficiently present your business or products to an audience that has been prescreened for what you offer. MVM on its own will never work in this face-to-face profession, but when it's paired with MLM and Mr. K's Rules, you've got an unstoppable force.

Building Your Master List

With Mr. K's Rules as your business development blueprint, let's look at how you build a database of potential distributor contacts. This detailed master list is the foundation of your business. As you compile it, be sure to safeguard your list using a system that gives you the information you need, exactly when you need it. In line with Organic Principle #3—Organization, I use a professional Contact Management System that allows me to capture the information needed for connecting with a particular person today or at a future date, regardless of where I am in the world on that day.

Another good reason for using a contact management system concerns the business cards you collect. Rifling through a big stack of cards to find that one you need is a time-waster, if ever there was one. Besides, Murphy's Law dictates that the business card you're looking for will always be at the bottom of the pile! Instead, get yourself a card scanner. This relatively inexpensive device turns hard copy information into a manageable online database. You can schedule and plan follow-ups with the ease of a mouse click. I also suggest you get into the habit of carrying a small notebook or using your smart phone to jot down any numbers or notes. Once you're back on your computer, you can easily transfer the information to your database.

Your master prospect list will consist of the three prospect categories. Load one hundred or more contacts into your database before making any calls!

- ❖ Your local list: Write down the names of seventy potential recruits or customers that live within your zip code or area code.

- ❖ Your national list: Identify twenty people who live somewhere in your country.

❖ Your international list: List ten people that reside anywhere in the world outside of your country.

Avoid editing as you compile your three lists. Remember, each person is a link to thousands of other contacts you would usually never be able to reach. If you don't give each person a chance, that link may be lost forever.

SIDEBAR: MEMORY JOGGERS

Here are some resources to help you build your three lists:

❖ High School yearbook   ❖ Friends in your social networks

❖ Family and friends   ❖ Massage therapist

❖ Neighbors   ❖ Personal trainer

❖ Doctor   ❖ Physiotherapist

❖ Dentist   ❖ Chiropractor

❖ Lawyer   ❖ Church members

❖ Current and past work colleagues   ❖ Association members (Rotary, BNI, Toastmasters, etc.)

Six Degrees of Separation

How did you feel when I asked you to put together these three lists? If you felt somewhat anxious, you're not alone. I have been told countless times, "But, I don't know one hundred people." Here are a couple of stories to help get you beyond that common myth.

In 1967, American social psychologist Stanley Milgram devised a new way to test a theory called, The Small-World Problem. He randomly selected people in the Midwestern United States;

these folks were asked to send a package to a total stranger living somewhere on the east coast, in Massachusetts. The senders were only given the intended recipient's name, occupation, and general location. They were then instructed to send the package to someone they knew on a first-name basis who was likely to know the intended package recipient. The theory was that a contact chain would be revealed. The Midwesterner would send the package to someone he knew, who would send the package on to someone she knew, and so on. Eventually the package would make it to its target.

Researchers expected that the chain would include at least one hundred intermediaries. Milgram's findings revealed that the delivery process averaged only five to seven contact points. More recent studies have recreated Milgram's concept on a global scale using email chains on the Internet. After reviewing the data collected, the number of digital intermediaries, from first sender to target recipient also averaged about six people. Milgram's findings are what gave rise to the phenomenon known as, Six Degrees of Separation.

In simplest terms, each of us are only about six people away from being connected to virtually every human being on the planet. As you compile your initial master list, recognize how significant every name is. Your list is your ability to connect with almost anyone in the world!

With the advent of social networking, planet Earth becomes your oyster. Do not be afraid of technology. Embrace it and squeeze out of it all the success you desire.

Building a Global Business

By the time I had reached Mr. K's 5th Rule and was earning more than $100,000 per month in sales and residual income, I became very keen on the idea of expanding my business to South Korea.

I was living in North America, at the time, and had no Korean contacts. To travel to Korea without any existing relationships would be a foolhardy and expensive decision on my part. I knew that if I wanted to build a distribution network based in Korea, I needed to expand my local network of contacts first.

Most cities have a diverse selection of ethnic-based publications that cater to immigrants and nationals who live or work outside of their country of origin. My plan was to first get connected within my local Korean business community and ultimately attract the local Korean contacts needed to assist me in expanding my business to their homeland. Here is the advertisement that I ran in the local Korean newspapers:

> U.S.-Based Company Expanding into Korea. We're looking for a few local entrepreneurs to help us with the launch of our company into Korea. Special Referral and Car bonuses available for qualified candidates. For more info call (888) 555-5555.

Because of this simple ad, I soon hooked up with a local Korean entrepreneur who was looking for a new business opportunity. Over the next several months, he and I met with members of the local Korean community to find other like-minded individuals. Our efforts paid off. We successfully recruited and sponsored a good group of locally-based Korean distributors, all of whom had contacts in Korea. My efforts to build the right team, locally, gave me the touch points to connect with potential distributors six thousand miles away.

Cultural Dos & Don'ts

When dealing with different cultures, the simplest mistakes can and will ruin a relationship, resulting in lost business opportunities. For example, many Asian cultures will react negatively to you making the OK gesture, giving the wrong gift, ignoring the ritual for the presentation of a business card, and not understanding their business hierarchy.

Once my local network began building contacts in Korea, I knew it was the right time to travel there and start the hands-on business building process. Organic Principle #11—Respect includes understanding and honoring diverse cultures and customs, something I have adhered to since I was a young teen. All too often I have seen visitors of one country treat the lifestyle differences of another country with disdain and rudeness. I was going to Korea to build a business, and in alignment with my Principle #11—Respect, I decided to study the cultural Dos and Don'ts of the Korean people before I stepped foot in their country.

Effective intercultural communication is a must in our global economy. As Organic Principle #8—Relationships tells us that business success has always been and will remain founded upon the understanding and nurturing of strong relationships. Over the years, and as a citizen of the world, I have connected with a variety of people from around the globe. From my experiences, I have developed the following checklist for building my own international sensitivity and knowledge of different cultural groups.

Before interacting with business people in another country, have a clear understanding of:

- General awareness of the country's history
- The importance of first impressions when you introduce and present yourself
- Language and phrases to avoid
- Male/Female roles
- Yes and No questions to avoid
- Rules of hierarchy

* Body language differences

* Gestures to avoid

* Physical contact and proximity boundaries

* Significance of eye contact and smiling

* Signs of hospitality

* Business etiquette

* Proper greeting (bow or handshake)

* Addressing others with respect

* Making appointments

* Business card presentations

* Time management and customs of punctuality

* Cultural differences regarding training for business success

* Apparel—offensive styles and colors to avoid

* Superstitions and taboos

* Negotiation customs

While finding this amount of information may seem a daunting task, it is critical that you develop a genuine feel for the culture of your new connections. This information will promote better communication, break down barriers, build trust, strengthen relationships, open opportunities and, in the long-run, yield positive, tangible results for your business.

Remember, one wrong move or simple misunderstanding may abruptly bring to a halt or delay your work for months. It is never wise to assume that other cultures are similar to our own.

Home Base Away from Home

When I arrived in Korea, armed with a thorough understanding of their cultural *Dos* and *Don'ts* and a list of contacts, I was ready to go to work! Guided by Principle #1—Readiness, one of the first things I did when I landed was to select a suitable accommodation to meet both my personal and business needs. The ideal facility had the following features:

- A central location, with easy access from all areas of the city

- Convenient parking for prospects and guests

- A dual-purpose room, with a separate living room and lounge area for conducting meetings

- Accessible business/meeting tools: Internet access, mobile, white board and markers, coffee, tea, and water

- Because I didn't speak any Hungal (Korean), I hired a good translator. With his help and the list I had built in North America, I started dialing the phone and contacting potential distributors. Every evening, we prepared for our work the following day, making sure that we had a plan in place for talking with prospects who were connected to the Korean distributors on my North American team.

This daily routine went on for nearly seven months. By the time I boarded the plane to fly home, I had successfully hit the goal of ten thousand distributors in Korea. But it didn't stop there. I went back to Korea fourteen times over the next two years to support my team.

Expanding my business into Korea is one of the most financially and personally rewarding decisions I've ever made. I was successful because of my unwavering commitment to following the rules and guidelines outlined in this chapter. If you follow Mr. K's Rules—building your database, demonstrating the drive and commitment necessary to expand your business, and respecting cultural Dos and Don'ts, your business can go from local to global in a very big way.

Chapter 11

HOW TO WINE AND DINE

When it comes to wining and dining in organic networking, I am a veteran. Over the last fifteen years, I have wined and dined team members, customers, and prospects as often as three times a week and sometimes more than once in the same day. This translates into thousands of breakfasts, lunches, dinners, and coffee meetings.

Everything shared in this chapter comes from real-life experience from my travels around the world. I have learned that I can increase my odds of business success if my intention for wining and dining is right and I have planned for the event properly. Organic Principal #1—Readiness comes into play here. Several times I have failed, and the reason was my lack of planning. Follow the guidelines in this chapter to minimize your failure rate.

Wining and Dining Today

Whenever we hear the phrase, Wine and Dine, we imagine some exotic restaurant where patrons feast on lobster and filet mignon while sipping some rare French wine. At the end of the evening, the waiter gives the check to the well-dressed man who arranged the dinner; he pays with his sky's-the-limit credit card, and then Mr. Well-Dressed departs with his guests in tow.

In the past, this traditional style of wining and dining was used frequently as a business tactic. The cost of an expensive steak dinner was the price you paid to nail down an order or lock in a special client. In today's environment, this formerly common practice has evolved into something much different. My goal in this chapter is to share with you the contemporary nuances of wining and dining.

We've all been wined and dined at some point in our lives, right? Some of those experiences were good, while others left a bad aftertaste in your mouth, and in your mind. So, what makes one wine-and-dine experience memorable and another an abysmal failure? It comes down to Principle #8—Relationships. You entertain prospects to set the stage for the nurturing of a relationship.

I see the psychology behind the wining and dining of a business client or network marketing prospect as very similar to the psychology of dating. You may think I have lost my mind with this outrageous comparison, but it's true. After all, there are good dates, bad dates, blind dates, spur-of-the-moment dates, and dates you would rather forget for the rest of your life. It's no different with business meetings. The psychology behind dating and business entertainment is the same and has always been a part of the human experience. It is all about satisfying one's need to be appreciated.

My comparison becomes even more significant when we consider the 3 Qs—the three types of prospects we'll encounter: Quantity, Quality, and Qualified. The Quality and Qualified groups are potentially the highest producers in our profession, and they will demand more personalized attention, recognition, and perks than the Quantity group. This is where my analogy between dating and doing business rings true. Your highest producers want to feel appreciated, and they expect you to wine and dine them as an acknowledgement of their contribution to your team.

ORGANICWISE:

Keep your wining and dining organic by staying grounded in genuine intentions. When it comes to impressing your prospects, especially from the Quality and Qualified groups, you need to be real. Never exaggerate or put on a front, since any encounter could turn into one of your most valued, long-term relationships.

Organic Wining and Dining

Wining and Dining sounds easy. However, it is not enough to pick a place, drive a few miles, and plop yourself in a meeting where you munch on a sandwich or sip coffee with someone you hardly know. There are certain steps and personal needs to consider as you develop your approach to wining and dining. For an organic networker, you are building new relationships. You just happen to be sharing a beverage or a meal at the same time.

Here is my organic process for building positive business relationships over the dinner table and at your favorite coffee shop:

- ❖ **Step 1. Find your Quality/Qualified Prospect**
  To build a long-term relationship for your business, you have to find the right prospect to do business with. That may sound simple, but isn't it better to wine and dine someone who is looking for what you and your company have to offer? You want a prospect who will buy into your vision and have the ability to support that vision over time.

❖ **Step 2. Plan your Meeting**

Before you invite a prospect to meet with you, plan when and where you will meet. Keep the venue low-key. Consider grabbing a coffee or do a breakfast meeting before work. Whatever you do, don't overdo it! Make the invitation sincere, and keep it simple.

❖ **Step 3. Start the Process of Romancing your Prospect**

Your first get-together with a prospect is a forum for getting to know each other. Using the dating metaphor, this encounter is akin to a casual first date where two people get acquainted. Find out their likes and dislikes. Learn about their family and occupation. Discover what recreational interests they have. These early meetings are a way of establishing a level of trust.

What you do not talk about is, money. Money is often considered a very personal subject, and you need to get to know someone reasonably well before you discuss income and financial goals. If your prospect broaches the subject of money, go ahead and talk about it, but be sensitive to how your prospect perceives money and topics of a financial nature.

❖ **Step 4. Romancing the Prospect**

Once you have established a comfortable, trust-based rapport with someone, which may take a few dates, you are ready to introduce your prospect to your business. Consider a lunch or a dinner for sharing this kind of information. Some cautionary advice: Be patient and do not expect him or her to sign up with your company immediately. Jumping into your arms overnight only happens in the movies. You are building a long-term, solid business relationship.

SIDEBAR: THE ORGANIC FLOW

Some prospects will become business friends faster than others. If a relationship isn't moving along as quickly as you'd like, be patient – Organic Principle #7—Patience. Abandoning one prospect for another is like giving up after one date. What if it takes someone a few dates to know and trust you? Avoid pursuing a prospect with lofty expectations. This usually leads to disappointment. Accept each individual for who he or she is and remain judgment-free.

As an organic progression of the relationship, introduce your prospect to what you enjoy doing. Laugh and keep the environment relaxed. Enjoy connecting for what it is—meeting people, socializing and spending time in the company of stimulating individuals.

❖ **Step 5. Nurture the Relationship**
By this step, you and your prospect have wined and dined a few times. You are both ready to make a more serious connection. If you were courting, this phase of dating would be when you decide to go steady!

In business, this is where the prospect may commit to try the products, attend some of your events, and perhaps meet with some of your business associates. Parallel to this would be introducing your new steady girlfriend or boyfriend to your parents. Remember, it is the trust that you have built over the previous days, weeks, and possibly months that fuels a prospect's interest in your business opportunity.

❖ **Step 6. Locking in the Relationship**
You have now reached the point where your prospect is prepared to make a real commitment. He or she is ready to fully engage in your support and your company's commitment to its distributors. Your prospect understands

your long-term vision and goals and is willing to invest time and resources to build with you.

As you can see, this entire organic process requires tremendous patience and fortitude.

In a nutshell, here is how you progressed through the preceding steps:

- ❖ You searched for the right person.

- ❖ You asked them out for a coffee and eventually to a dinner.

- ❖ You got to know each other.

- ❖ Finally, you reached a level of trust and commitment to work together.

Building Trust

At any point in my daily business-building activities, I have anywhere between thirty and forty Quality or Qualified prospects in my pipeline. Wining and dining does not mean spending large amounts of money to entice these potential prospects. I balance the trust-building steps and the appropriate amount of entertainment resources I choose to apply. In other words, a network marketer doesn't have to spend beyond his or her means. The goal of the organic process is to build trust and positive relationships through meaningful and enjoyable wine-and-dine experiences.

SIDEBAR: WINING AND DINING THE OPPOSITE SEX

In order to avoid any misunderstanding or inaccurate expectations, I always advise my distributors to follow these guidelines:

- ❖ When inviting a man/woman to meet with you, invite him/her to bring his significant other along.

- ❖ Pick a location with a business atmosphere, rather than an intimate environment.

- ❖ Choose a time during business hours, rather than in the late evening.

- ❖ Dress conservatively and address appropriate topics.

A few years ago, I had coffee with a prospect. During the meeting, I noticed what kind of pastry he enjoyed. Several days later I went to my favorite bakery, ordered his favorite pastry, and hand-delivered it to his house. Needless to say, his family was thrilled with the gift. My visit gave me the opportunity to meet and connect with his family in a way that would not have been possible at a business meeting.

However, over time, we did build a relationship based on trust. To forego my thoughtful, organic approach in favor of forcing an outcome is not only the wrong tactic, it invariably fails and often taints the reputation of the pursuer. Therefore, I am willing to be patient.

Chapter 12

TRAVEL AND ENTERTAINMENT SECRETS

I was speaking recently with a business associate on the topic of hotel guest programs and airline frequent-flyer programs. Within minutes I was rattling off all the benefits of my current airline program and commenting on how easy it was to get free flights and upgrade vouchers. My friend said, "Kosta, you are a wealth of knowledge in this area. You should share what you know with others." That conversation was my motivation for writing this chapter.

Competition for customers has never been as fierce as it is today for the airline companies. That's why most of them offer incentive programs, commonly called, loyalty programs. Consumers have more choices and the value of a customer-loyalty program has the power to make or break a business. The vast number of programs available, coupled with your ability to select the right companies, is what will complement your organic networking objectives.

Loyalty Programs

When loyalty programs are initiated by airlines, hotels, restaurants, and other retailers, there are always two major goals in mind. The primary goal is the acquisition of information about a customer's spending habits. The secondary goal is an organic one. They want to cultivate loyalty, ensuring that a customer continues to patronize their business.

Many programs offer a sustained discount, such as 10 percent, for a period of time, perhaps for a year, perhaps for the life of the business. Others offer a discount once certain criteria have been met. For example, once a customer has spent two hundred dollars on merchandise or services, a 20 percent discount may be offered on a single purchase. Other companies offer points to be redeemed on products that may or may not be directly related to the business. One of the reasons loyalty programs are so successful is that they offer the customer something that is, or appears to be, essentially free.

SIDEBAR: LOYALTY PLUSES

Reduce Costs: Your loyalty gets you free perks instead of paying for a product or service.

- ❖ Leverage Supplier Relationships: When it comes to requesting complimentary perks, the more business you give them, the more leverage you'll have.

- ❖ Provide Consistency: The benefits of Principle #4—Consistency applies to vendor-client relationships, too. You know what companies you can count on.

Since loyalty programs are about building a relationship, you want to choose companies that are dedicated to giving you the best possible customer experience. This is an important criterion, whether you are booking a flight, redeeming hotel reward points, or simply calling about a customer service issue. A company with a good loyalty program will go out of its way to build a two-way dialogue with you. This is done by integrating rewards in ways that innately boost engagement. In exchange for your loyalty, these companies will, then, provide you with free perks, such as merchandise or discounts not enjoyed by the general population of customers they support.

Loyalty programs have increased in popularity over the past fifteen years, in no small part due to the development of a culture of entitlement. Consumers today feel they deserve special treatment. Businesses capitalize on this culture by offering benefits that cost them little but bring the customer an assumed prestige. This could come in the form of access to an express line at check-in or valet parking.

Choose Your Perks

Rewards from loyalty programs generally fall into these categories:

- Points and Cash Back

- Discounted Fee or Fee Elimination

- Third Party Merchant Discounts

- Financial Credit

- Preferential Treatment and Recognition

Faced with these exciting options, the last thing you want to do, as an organic networker, is to start signing up for every program you can find. In any supplier or merchant relationship, the decision to buy what they have to offer must be motivated by how well it serves your business.

For example, let's say that Airline A and Airline B both service the cities you wish to travel to. Airline A may have the best frequent flyer program in North America, but they only fly in and out of an airport that is two hundred miles from where you live. Airline B has a hub at an airport twenty minutes from your house. Does it make business sense to join Airline A's loyalty program? Not really, because you would be wasting valuable time to get to Airline A's departure point when Airline B is far more convenient.

When it comes to earning perks, remember that the important word is earn. You spend money in order to earn something in return. The more you spend, the greater the potential for earning rewards. Here are some of the different types of merchants and the types of rewards you can capitalize on.

- Credit Cards: Points redemption and/or transfer, cash rebates, merchandise vouchers

- Airlines: Points redemption for flights, merchandise or hotels, upgrade vouchers, lounge access

- Rental Car Companies: Airline mileage credits, free rentals, vehicle upgrades

- Restaurants and Coffee Chains: Wine, beverage, and meal credits; card stamping for return customers; get-one-free offers

- Hotels: Airline mileage credit, points redeemed for free nights, upgrade vouchers, and meal credits

- Department Stores: Points redemption, gift certificate redeemable on next purchase

- Casinos: Swipe card points for redemption on food, beverages, and accommodations

---

ORGANICWISE:

Building relationships with your vendors is an organic process. That's Principle #8—Relationships. It may take time to reach the top rewards level in a frequent flyer program, at least in your first couple of years as an organic networker. That's okay. Build slowly to build big! Other loyalty programs, like the ones you find in coffee chains, start paying off within the first few times you purchase products.

Maximize the Relationships

Once you have selected the suppliers that meet your business requirements, there are certain steps to be taken to build and maximize your relationships. My experience in this area relates to airlines, hotels, credit cards, and restaurants, but my guidelines can be applied to any merchant that offers a loyalty program.

Hotels

Every major hotel chain is looking for customers who book rooms in their properties on a frequent basis. If you know you'll be travelling for your business and that you will be meeting clients and potentially holding meetings at these locations, select a hotel that reflects the lifestyle, budget, and image you wish to convey. Avoid staying in small hotel chains or boutique hotels. They are extremely limited when it comes to locations and offer few options when it comes to earning upgrades and free-night stays.

Find a hotel chain that has properties in the cities you will be traveling to, and confirm in advance that they meet your business needs – Organic Principle #1—Readiness. Study their loyalty program, and make sure you understand how you will be rewarded in return for your business. Get to know the recognition thresholds of their loyalty plan so that you can earn a position at the top of their customer recognition and perks list. Then, support that chain in the following ways:

- ❖ Book all of your overnight stays with them.

- ❖ Use their meeting rooms, if needed.

- ❖ Use their restaurant for your meals and entertainment.

Marriott offers one of the best customer loyalty and recognition programs in the hospitality industry. Their extremely rewarding, multi-tier system motivates you to want to get to their top tier sooner, rather than later. I learned this lesson from one of my mentors, who was a loyal Marriott member for years. Every time we travelled together, his rooms were always upgraded to suites, with free access to private lounges. I had to pay for these privileges when I was traveling with him! If I wanted to take advantage of those perks and upgrades, I needed to follow his lead and reach the top tier, as well. And that's what I did.

A few years later, when I started holding my meetings in Toronto, I stayed loyal to Marriott and was automatically advanced to their highest level after hosting several events with them in one year. I was treated as a VIP and offered upgrades and access to those private lounges, too. Those perks enabled me to wine and dine my clients and enjoy my travels more than ever. After all, if you're going to travel, why not reap the benefits of those loyalty programs?

Airlines

What the airlines want to see from you, in order to pass along the perks is, frequency, hence the familiar term, Frequent Flyer programs. As I mentioned, the airline you choose must be a good fit with your logistic needs. Read through the benefits of each airline's Frequent Flyer program and learn how to maximize mileage in a way that complements your business travel obligations. As with hotels, be aware of the recognition levels you need to attain in order to gain a top position on their list of customers who earn rewards and perks.

Reap the benefits of reaching a top-tier position by supporting your chosen airline or airlines in the following ways:

- Book all your business travel with them.
- Use their airline-branded credit card.
- Fly during incentive periods for extra miles.
- Stay in hotels that reward you with your airline's travel miles.
- Rent cars that reward you with your airline's travel miles.
- Donate air miles to airline-supported charities.
- Book your holiday travel on the same airline.

As your organic networking business grows from local to national and then global, you will reach the point where you are traveling by air several times a year. If you plan to take your family with you, purchase your own ticket and use points to fly your loved ones. This allows you to continue accumulating miles, even as you use mileage, and it progresses you toward the airline's top customer tier. Over the years, I have earned millions of air travel miles. I did this by using only a small handful of airlines and I reached the top tier of every one of them.

Car Rentals

If you rent a car when you travel, do your utmost to make your reservations with the same company. Rental car companies have a much lower threshold for top tier status than airlines or hotels. Whenever it makes business sense, replace short flights with car rental driving, especially in the early months of the year. That way, you can benefit from top tier status for the rest of the year.

Credit Cards

There are many fee-for-services credit cards that offer points programs and align themselves with a variety of merchants. In some situations, credit cards also offer cash rebates. The criteria for selecting a loyalty program credit card should be based upon a flexible points plan that offers a variety of options:

- Multiple Airline Rewards

- Points Balance Transfer to other Programs

- Cash Rebates

- Car Rental Insurance

- Delayed Flight Insurance

- Baggage Loss Coverage

- Accident Insurance

- Promotional Airline and Merchant Vouchers

- Family Discounts and Travel Incentives

- Access to Airline Travel Lounges

As always, choose a credit card that matches up with your business objectives. It's even better for your business if you get benefits for consolidating all of your spending purchases with that credit card company.

SIDEBAR: AIM FOR ZERO

Loyalty program credit cards will charge high interest rates. The best balance to carry on these cards is a Zero balance. Pay off your credit card in full every month to avoid high interest charges that can accumulate quickly!

Restaurants

While the number of restaurants offering loyalty programs is much lower than with airlines and hotels, they are out there. Sometimes all you need to do is ask, like checking to see if you can connect a free meeting room with your purchase of coffee and tea during a meeting. As Principle #5—Initiative tells us, it always pays to be proactive, even when it comes to negotiating a deal with the restaurant manager.

In the community where I live, for example, we hold our annual homeowners' association meeting at a local restaurant. They have an excellent meeting room that we get for free, provided that we spend one hundred dollars in the restaurant. Our board members hold their quarterly review in the restaurant before the general meeting. It is never a problem for the seven-member board to spend a hundred dollars on food so that we get the free room.

When I was living in Vancouver, Canada, I consistently used the same hair stylist, spa, group of restaurants, and many other suppliers. This enabled me to build a great relationship with the management staff and get VIP treatment. Today, I'm following the same path, practicing what I'm preaching to you. From the limo company to the hotel used for my business guests and for my personal needs, everything is done using the same vendors every time. This gives me leverage to bypass lines, get the best seats in the house, enjoy the best service, and take advantage of the many other perks that come with being a loyal customer.

As you plan your travel and entertainment for business, consider how your participation in a loyalty program can reduce your costs or permit you to enjoy perks that you would not normally be able to afford. The more effectively you reinforce the needs of your organic networking business with the right loyalty programs, the more they will contribute to your overall success.

Chapter 13

HOW TO CONDUCT SUCCESSFUL EVENTS

When I talk to people looking at opportunities in network marketing, a common complaint I hear is that someone walked away from a company's second presentation more confused than they were after the first meeting. When I ask for details, these prospects often tell me that they went to a first presentation, returned the following week, and found that the two presentations had very little in common. This inconsistency flies in the face of Principle #4—Consistency.

I did just about everything wrong when it came to planning meetings. Three months into my business, my mentor attended yet another unsuccessful meeting I was conducting. After the meeting, he took me aside for a late night talk. He critiqued me, honestly, telling me what he'd noticed about my meeting skills. I, in turn, took twenty pages of notes.

It was two o'clock in the morning, when I arrived home. I was exhausted and a bit discouraged. However, I was also excited to test and apply what I had learned that night. As tired as I was, I couldn't sleep. I wondered what could have happened, had I met with him on Day 1, instead of Day 90.

In the morning, I decided to put his suggestions to work, requesting a meeting with my leadership the very next night. After running through what I had learned, my team leaders were galvanized. We implemented my mentor's advice and, within a few months, we saw dramatic improvement. About eighteen months later, the new meeting system had become the standard for that company across the country.

The Organic Franchise Model

I have since taken my mentor's valuable insights and designed a method of operation for meetings that I call, The Organic Franchise Model. My system is one of the core ingredients of my success. In fact, I have mastered this system so thoroughly that I was asked to co-author another book on the subject. Why does this matter? Your message to distributors and prospects not only needs to be clearly presented at your meetings, the basic setup and content of the meetings must also be consistent. This standard applies, no matter where your presentations take place or who the presenters are.

Network marketing is not a franchise business; you don't have to invest millions to get started, for one. But the analogy works when it comes to running meetings and events. Let's look at a franchise model known around the world, McDonald's. Have you ever wondered how McDonald's can be so successful when teenagers and retirees appear to run their stores? It's simple. McDonald's has an amazing system in place. Customers order food, pick up their meals, grab their condiments, sit down and eat, drop off their trays, and leave. The entire process takes about twenty minutes. As an added plus, the customer knows the basic menu items and advertised specials before walking in or pulling up to the drive-thru.

If someone isn't sure what to order, there's always the big, easy-to-read menu board.

Now, imagine what would happen to sales if the McDonald's in every city had a different menu. You'd arrive at a McDonald's in Seattle and maybe they'd serve a salmon burger, instead of your favorite fish sandwich. Or maybe a New York franchise would serve pizza, while a location in Tucson offered tacos. Variety can be a good thing, but McDonald's never confuses its customers. Anywhere you go in the world, while you may find subtle variances, McDonald's menu offerings are consistent. This franchise business has mastered systemization!

Trust the System

My Organic Franchise Model is also based on systemization. By following this system, you will have a consistent plan in place for generating maximum productivity for each and every meeting. Here are some systemization guidelines:

- ❖ **Timing Is Everything.** Plan your meeting for a time of day when potential attendees are most likely to be available. The best times do not interfere with normal business hours and family time.

- ❖ **Invite the Right People.** You learned about the 3 Qs of Recruiting. Although all 3 Qs are necessary for building your business, invite the people who will most benefit from understanding the potential of your business opportunity— Quality and Quantity prospects. They are vitally important to the organic growth of your business and the lifeblood of any organization for long-term success.

- ❖ **Set a Specific Goal.** Meetings will be more productive when attendees know exactly why the meeting has been scheduled and which specific goals are to be accomplished.

❖ **Stay On Track.** People lose interest when a meeting veers off track. Stick to your agenda and meeting timeline. If off-topic ideas or questions come up, keep a *parking lot list* so that you can continue with the agenda without losing useful ideas that can be addressed later.

ORGANICWISE:

The Organic Franchise Model systemizes your events, beginning with your first meeting and duplicating organically as you build your team of distributors. You can rely on consistency across the organization. Strong roots lead to strong branches!

Prepare to Dazzle

I was told long ago that an audience will take in 10 percent of what is being communicated from my words, 20 percent from my delivery style, and 70 percent from nonverbal cues and body language. In other words, the presenter and the presentation style are more important than the actual words used. Top concentration-killers in meetings tend to fall into these categories: poor speaking skills, like a flat, monotone voice; repetition; over-gesturing; overusing industry buzzwords; lack of direction; and physical discomfort.

To keep your meeting participants energized and engaged, try these tips for holding your audience's attention:

❖ **Room Size:** Make sure that the room you've booked is comfortable and matches to the number of participants you expect. Using a big room designed for one hundred people for a group of fifteen folks will be as uncomfortable as stuffing one hundred people into a room appropriate for only fifteen individuals.

❖ **Use humor:** Tell a joke, a funny story, or a personal experience related to the meeting topic. Or open your presentation with an amusing slide or famous quote.

❖ **Pose a question:** Ask a question early in the meeting, but tell participants that you don't want an answer until the end. To encourage active listening, hint that you'll offer a small prize for the first correct answer.

❖ **Engage participants:** I can't emphasize this enough. Use eye contact to draw people in.

❖ **Get personal:** Give credit to participants when they offer certain facts, statistics, and ideas. Encourage distributors to offer details of their involvement or accomplishments.

❖ **Show and tell:** Use visuals to get your point across. Spark things up with a hands-on demonstration or PowerPoint graphics. Use a variety of visual tools to keep things fresh.

❖ **Unlock the mystery:** Abstract concepts and statistics will cause eyes to glaze over. Use real-world examples to provide an understandable comparison or explain a key point. When possible, relate the numbers to the participants' personal lives.

❖ **Snappy ending:** Don't bog down the end of your meeting with repetitive comments and summarizing. I usually close by asking open-ended questions that relate to the topic of the meeting. A successful, snappy ending leaves people motivated to take action in whatever direction you've guided them to go.

Planning Your Meeting

When I started building my team, in 2001, we had nothing but a dream. At our first meeting, only two people showed up, myself and one other presenter. At our second meeting, we had one guest in the room, bringing the total to a whopping three attendees. Not much to get excited about, however, we did have a 33 percent increase in attendance!

Slowly, over a period of weeks and months, attendance continued to grow. Three years later, my network marketing meetings averaged from seventy to one hundred people each. This was also true for the established weekly business meetings in cities all over Canada. At international meetings, the numbers of attendees can be in the thousands.

My goal was to grow my business, and the secret to my success was the consistency of my meeting plan. By committing to the Organic Franchise Model, I knew that a distributor in Toronto could send a Florida-based prospect to a meeting in Miami, knowing with confidence that his prospect would receive consistent and accurate information. The Miami meeting would start on time and follow the appropriate agenda within the allotted time frame.

So, in the spirit of Principle #1—Readiness, let's examine the Organic Franchise Model for planning and running a successful organic networking event.

* **Meeting Setup.** A registration table should be placed just outside the meeting room and manned by a few volunteers from the team. These greeters need to be ready to serve the new guests coming in.

  A product display table should be set up at the front of the room.

  Presenters should review the slides and be prepared to provide the same high-quality, standardized information heard at other similar meetings across town or across the country.

❖ **The Agenda.** Whether you sell products or services, and no matter which compensation plan your business offers, a successful meeting agenda should consist of the following three sections and a closing call to action. This ensures that audiences are given the full-spectrum overview of your company.

❖ **Section 1: Product Overview and Testimonial.** Following opening comments, the presenter will review the agenda for the meeting. Next, in clear and simple terms, the presenter will review the details of the product or service being presented. This includes the features, benefits, and advantages of the products.

Following the product overview, the presenter will invite prearranged guests or distributors to share their personal experience about the product or service. These testimonials are an excellent way to validate the features and benefits.

❖ **Section 2: Business Opportunity Overview.** This is the main section of the meeting. Depending upon the company's format and marketing strategy, this area will differ in content. I have attended many meetings in this profession, and for the most part, the Business Opportunity Overview will highlight these key areas:

  ❖ **Leadership and Corporate Overview.** This segment focuses on the company owners and field leadership.

  ❖ **Compensation Plan.** This is a brief overview of the distributor compensation plan, including the main income streams for new distributors as they grow their businesses.

  ❖ **Support Systems.** The presenter describes the support systems developed by the company. These are the systems that permit all distributors to replicate and duplicate the company-provided system for building a team.

❖ **Section 3: Timing.** In this section, the presenter will describe how current market conditions affect the desirability of the opportunity. This ties into the prospects' awareness of their own personal situations and presents the value of making a decision sooner, rather than later.

❖ **The Close: Call to Action.** Finally, you introduce a call to action, enabling meeting attendees to either sign up now or get their questions answered. Upon the conclusion of the formal meeting, one of the leaders will usually hold a mini meeting immediately afterwards, and he or she can explain the compensation package more fully to those who are interested.

Setting Up the Perfect Environment

Of course, there's more to the business meeting than having confidence in the plan, the presentation, and the quality of information. Your appearance is important when it comes to meeting new prospects. I find it so important that I have standardized that all prospects and guests be courteously greeted by current distributors dressed in business attire.

Unifying the presentations also involves some basic logistics for the setup of the meeting room. For example, since distributors and guests usually enter through doors at the back of the room, I make sure that the main presentation activities take place at the front of the room. That way, late arrivals can walk in without disrupting the presentation.

There is always uplifting, energetic music playing, from the time the doors open to the time the actual business presentation begins. This helps create an enthusiastic, upbeat atmosphere that gets people into a receptive and positive mindset.

The meeting room always includes a water station that is replenished about halfway through the meeting. Dehydration diminishes concentration, so I make sure to keep water on hand. Like the water cooler at the office, the water station is also a place for distributors and their guests to socialize. However, I simply ask that any conversations take place before and after the business meeting, not during it.

An organic networker also has respect for the hotel hosts. Bills are paid on time, and the hotel staff is treated in a courteous manner by our leaders and distributors. Without the hotel facilities and their support staff, I'd be constantly looking for a place to hold formal business meetings, as well as those essential after-the-meeting meetings, when a distributor and a prospect can really talk on a more personal, detailed level.

The Organic Franchise Model for organic networking builds consistency into meetings on a local, national, and global scale. The consistency factor also goes a long way when it comes to building and unifying a team. After all, that's what makes organic networking such a dynamic opportunity. You build a team, then go above and beyond to help them succeed. And that leads to lifetime residuals.

SECTION FOUR
PERSONAL DEVELOPMENT

While it may seem like an ambitious undertaking, becoming a life manager and a master communicator is simply an organic process. You learn certain skills, you practice them, and you excel.

Chapter 14

MANAGING TIME IN YOUR LIFE

There is no business or profession in the world, if you want to grow, that will not require you to learn to manage time and not let time manage you. I strongly believe that we need to continually learn from the best in the industry, and in my opinion, one of the best, when it comes to time management, is Brian Tracy. His materials have been invaluable to me in building my business.

The last time I checked, there were only sixty seconds in a minute, sixty minutes in an hour, and twenty-four hours in a day. These finite chunks of time have not changed for centuries. I've learned that the real secret to time management has nothing to do with how you manage time. It is more about how you utilize time as part of your life management. Organic Principle #3—Organization focuses on how to manage our life and what we do with the time we have.

Over the years, I have learned to focus on life management, rather than trying to manage time, and it has helped to get me from where I started in organic networking to where I am today. I have developed some tried-and-true skills for improving productivity by 25 percent, on a day-to-day basis, that includes four direct benefits:

* **Gain Twelve Minutes per Hour.** By truly applying my *12 Organic Principles for Success*, they could help you save hundreds of productive hours per year.

  If gaining twelve minutes per hour sounds like small change, do the math:

  12 minutes/hour x 8 hours/day x 5 days/week x 52 weeks/year = 416+ productive, profitable hours a year!

  Consider what you could do with ninety extra minutes per day and how much that time is worth to you.

* **Increase Your Net Worth by 20 Percent.** Ask any successful entrepreneur and they will agree that time is money. If you could free up ninety productive minutes per day, imagine the potential benefit of being able to increase your net worth by almost 20 percent.

* **12 Minutes Per Hour = 90 Minutes Per Day.** Think about what you could do with 90 extra minutes each day. How many new contacts or sales calls could you make? How about working out, playing golf, or enjoying a hobby that always seems to get put on the back burner? In today's busy world, we can all use extra time each day to charge ahead with our business or just chill out with a good book, relax, work out, run errands, or go to a movie.

* **Ability to Balance Personal and Business Life.** You can't put a price tag on being able to spend more time with the people you care about the most. When I was working seven days a week to build my business, the ninety extra minutes allowed me time to enjoy a long walk with my significant other or have lunch with a friend.

Becoming a successful network marketer is more than working; it's about life management – finding the balance between work, family, and friends.

10 Daily Rituals to Help Manage Your Time

Those 90 extra minutes are invaluable when you adopt daily rituals that allow you to organize your time and be more productive, personally and in building your business. The objective is to change your behavior, not allowing time to control you, in order to achieve the goals you've set for yourself. What becomes apparent, once you focus on life management and it begins to change your behavior, is that you will learn to set specific goals and align your time commitments against those goals.

These 10 Daily Rituals will help you develop new behaviors that increase productivity on a day-to-day basis.

* ❖ **Choose the Right Tools.** The first step is analyzing where your time is spent, now. Then, you plan how you're going to spend your time in the future. For that, you need the right tools for the job. Many people use a notebook-style calendar and carry it with them at all times. Others use their computer, laptop, or cell phone. There are software programs that enable you to schedule events and set reminders. I use a mobile app that syncs my computer calendar with my smart phone. If you have a smart phone, have you learned all the time management features loaded on it? If not, what are you waiting for?

  Finding the right calendar tool will go a long way toward making the time management process easier. Of course, this kind of ease depends upon how diligently you load your appointments and meetings into your calendar and keep track of your activities. Principle #2—Discipline can serve you well in this area.

I recommend you review your To-Do list at the beginning of each day and identify what you must get accomplished. For starters, try to keep the must-dos to three or less per day and focus on getting them done. At the end of the day, you'll feel proud of what you've accomplished, no matter what is left undone.

* **Don't Stretch Yourself Too Thin.** The reason so many new network marketers burn out is that they stretch themselves too thin, believing they can do it all. They work full-time, commute a couple of hours daily, spend quality time with their family and friends, do volunteer and committee work, get involved in causes, race to the gym five days a week in an effort to stay fit and healthy, and spend very little time relaxing or rejuvenating themselves. I get exhausted just thinking about it!

Decide what roles and activities are most important to you, and start implementing them immediately.

* **Set Priorities.** Another part of the do-it-all balancing act is the idea that everything is equally important. However, that's untrue. Look at your calendar on any given day. Is picking up the dry-cleaning really as important as calling that prospect? What's more beneficial to your organic marketing success, running errands or running meetings?

* **Delegate the To-Dos.** When you are in the startup stages of building a network marketing business, understand that you need to let other people carry some of the load. It is okay to ask your upline for help. They know much more than you do and are happy to do followups, training, business meetings, and assist you in designing a recruiting campaign. Think of all the different business-related tasks you perform in a single week. List them and prioritize them, then determine how much time you need to spend on each task to move your business forward. For example,

how many hours did you spend on administrative duties versus calling new prospects? If someone else can do that paperwork, it's time to delegate.

* **Don't Let the Time Bandits Rob You.** Time bandits steal precious minutes that can add up to hours that can be used more productively. Who are your time bandits? Do you spend too much time surfing the net, reading email, texting, or making personal calls? Make a commitment to eliminate your personal time bandits. For example, for one week, make it a goal that you'll not take personal phone calls while you're working. Let personal calls go to voicemail, and return them during a break.

Remember, the focus of time management is changing your behaviors so that you can manage all aspects of your life.

* **Learn to Say, Yes and No.** To become successful in life you must learn to say, no. Instead of saying, no, people will often say, maybe. In business and your personal life, maybe, is an indecisive word that causes an incredible amount of misunderstanding and frustration and creates expectation on the part of the recipient. How many times have networkers with leadership potential quit because they were always solving someone else's problems because they couldn't say, no? Make it a standard policy that it isn't your responsibility to solve your downline's problems.

Make it a general rule to delete, maybe, from your vocabulary. Instead, learn to make quicker decisions by saying, yes or no. Don't get hung up on elaborating a convoluted reason for your decision because you used the word, maybe. A simple, "No, I can't do that," is enough. People will appreciate your honesty and the fact that you don't want them wasting your valuable time. You'll also be free from the pressure to fit someone else's to-do into your schedule.

SIDEBAR: WHAT TYPE OF TIME MANAGER ARE YOU?

The Firefighter: Every event is a crisis. Tasks pile up around you, while you spend the day rushing from fire to fire.

The Over-Committer: Your answer to every request is, yes. You're so busy that you don't know what to do first. You are the one hiding in the restroom, overwhelmed by too many to-dos.

Mr. / Ms. Cool: You're too laid-back to complete tasks or return calls. Getting to things when you can get around to them isn't time management; it's avoidance. You're the one with your feet on your desk when you need to get busy!

The Motor Mouth: Born to socialize, you can't resist exercising your verbal skills at every opportunity. Each interaction becomes a long, drawn-out conversation, especially if there's an unpleasant, deadline-driven task on your calendar. You probably answered your cell phone while reading this chapter.

The Perfectionist: Exact is your middle name. Finishing tasks to your satisfaction is such a problem that you need more time zones, not just more time. You need to remember we are all perfectly imperfect!

The Procrastinator: You live by the mantra that anything worth doing is worth putting off. Hooked on drama or adrenaline, you'd rather rush to finish a task at the last minute. You know you have to stop procrastinating, but you'll probably change this behavior—you guessed it—tomorrow.

❖ **Establish Routines.** While a crisis may arise occasionally, you will be more productive if you follow simple, established routines most of the time. A sense of routine and order will help you develop a stronger focus.

❖ **Set Your Limits.** Manage your technology, instead of being managed by it! Reading and answering emails can eat up your entire morning, if you let it. Instead, set a limit of one hour per day for emails and stick to this routine. You also don't have to answer every phone call or let incoming texts or tweets interrupt your task at hand. I set aside particular times in my day to respond to messages or voicemails.

Here is where you must draw the line. It is unproductive for you to be reachable and connected all of the time. In fact, there are times when it's important to be unreachable to anyone except the person or the task immediately in front of you. Recognize when it is appropriate for you to unplug.

❖ **Organize Your Systems.** Do you ever waste time looking for a certain document? Have you ever spent twenty minutes trying to find an old email? Is your paper filing system slowing you down? Take the time to organize your documents and email folders. Redo your filing systems to the point that you can quickly get your hands on what you need, and commit to maintaining the improved systems.

❖ **Take Time Off.** The success of your business depends on what you do, not on how much time you spend doing it. Some people believe the more time they spend building their business, the more successful they will become. Before they know it, they're working seven days a week and wondering why they feel so tired and frazzled all the time. I encourage you to plan for and incorporate blocks of free time into your schedule. When you take time for yourself, whether it's an afternoon or a Saturday off, you'll return to your work refreshed and more productive.

A Day in the Life

I want to share some of the life management techniques that I adopted to gain those additional ninety minutes each day. The examples I use are real, as they come from one of my calendar pages in 2002. I can remember the specific day as if it were yesterday! While I was quite organized, even back then, I used my work time less effectively than I do now.

8am – 8:30am

Then: I spent this time planning the day. In those days, I never made a call to a potential prospect or distributor before 8:30am (Time wasted: thirty minutes)

Today: I plan my next day—a cumulative process of booking appointments and meetings—the day before, at the latest. This opens thirty minutes at the beginning of each day for making calls or having coffee with a prospect.

8:30am – 9:20am

Then: I made my first telephone calls. Only one of the calls with a new prospect was productive, and we booked another appointment. I made other calls but always got voicemails so I left messages asking people to call me back when they had a chance.

While leaving a voicemail message with one person, I missed a return phone call. This resulted in playing phone tag.

Around 9:30am, I called a prospect, and he answered. I started a conversation without asking if it was a good time to talk. After he listened to me for five minutes, he cut in and said he had to go to a meeting and asked that I call him back in the afternoon. I said I would, and we hung up. (Time wasted: about twenty minutes)

Today: While I am not going to reach everyone on the first call, playing phone tag can be a serious time-waster. Today, I schedule call times in advance. When I have to leave a message, I include a specific callback time so that the person can reach me more easily.

Also, when I make a cold call or a call that has not been pre-arranged, I immediately ask if it is a good time to talk for "X" number of minutes. If the person tells me, no, or asks that I call him back later, we set a specific time for the callback.

9:20am – 9:35am

Then: I took a personal call from a buddy of mine who wanted to go over plans for next weekend's birthday party for a mutual friend. (Time wasted: fifteen minutes)

Today: I should have let this call go to voicemail or told my friend that I'd call him back in the evening. Today, I designate specific times for personal calls during non-primetime hours or in the evening.

10am – 10:15am

Then: After making some additional calls, I suddenly remembered that I hadn't ordered samples for an upcoming meeting that had been scheduled a week ago. I placed the order. (Time wasted: fifteen minutes)

Today: It never pays to procrastinate! I place orders as soon as the date of a meeting has been established.

10:30am – 2pm

Then: After pulling my materials together, I drove two hours to meet a prospect. I got there ten minutes late due to a big traffic jam, only to discover that my prospect had an emergency and couldn't make our appointment. Because I had only planned one meeting in this area, the only choice I had was to head back home. It started to snow heavily on the drive back and all I could think about was that I was ready to throw in the towel. (Time wasted: 210 minutes)

Today: It always pays to confirm an appointment prior to departure. Emergencies happen and prospects with full-time jobs sometimes need to cancel. Today, I confirm appointments and pay attention to traffic reports so that I can forecast possible delays.

2pm – 4:30pm

Then: When I finally got home despite the fact that the day had been a struggle up to this point, I got on a roll. Over the next two hours, I confirmed two new distributor enrollments and booked three additional prospects for opportunity meetings. Finally, the day was starting to show some promise!

Today: Organic Principle #6—Persistence always pays off! As much as I felt like I had wasted a lot of time that morning, I buckled down and made calls. This has been my attitude for years and a primary reason that I have achieved great success.

4:30pm – 5:05pm

Then: I made a quick dash to the dry cleaners to pick up my slacks. It suddenly dawned on me that I had driven past the dry cleaners on my way home from that canceled appointment. (Time wasted: thirty-five minutes)

Today: I organize my day in advance, always strategizing how to optimize my time. If I know I have an appointment in another town, I make sure that other to-dos in the area can be done.

That day, back in 2002, ended with a successful evening meeting. When I look back, my day had a few high points. But, I also wasted over five hours. Frankly, I can barely remember the last time I had such an unproductive day! I'm certain you can see how easily I could have found at least a few extra hours.

ORGANICWISE:

To manage the time of your life organically, begin by creating a system that allows you to be fully prepared.

❖ Always plan your day in advance, the night before at the very latest.

❖ Prioritize from the most important to the least important task.

❖ Organize your tasks by location.

❖ Allocate the amount of time required for each task.

❖ Revisit your plan in the morning and confirm, add, or cancel tasks.

❖ Limit emailing and reading mail, and make sure that time has been prescheduled.

Mind Your Time

Over the years, and in the spirit of Organic Principle #3— Organization, I have developed particular time guidelines for full-time and part-time organic networkers. Apply this system as appropriate to your time commitment per week.

❖ **Full-Time Organic Networkers**

9am to 12 noon: Make and retrieve phone calls and follow-ups.

12 noon to 1pm: Enjoy lunch.

1pm to 5pm: Get your daily tasks done.

5pm to 6pm: Rest and enjoy dinner.

6pm to 10pm: Do your recruiting activities.

* **Part-Time Organic Networkers**

(Working three hours per day, four to five days per week)

One hour for follow-up activities—calls, emails

One hour for recruiting activities

One hour for getting your work-related tasks done

Within each day, there are primetime and non-primetime slots. These slots guide you as to when it's best to schedule certain organic networking activities. Whether you work three hours a week or 40+ hours a week, these guidelines should influence how you schedule your business activities.

* **Primetime Duties: 9am – 12 noon or 6pm – 9pm**

Team follow-ups

Recruiting new prospects

Meeting new prospects

* **Non-Primetime Duties: 1pm – 5pm**

Email/Social media

Product delivery

Meeting existing distributors at home or corporate office for follow-ups

Daily non-business-related tasks

Organic Approach to Building

There is a significant benefit that comes with utilizing a system to build your business versus relying solely on one-on-one meetings. While both are necessary elements of a successful approach, a systemized, organic approach will save you time.

In an organic approach, do the following from your home office:

* Connect the prospect to a live or recorded webinar so that he or she can get a brief overview of the company (5 minutes)

* Direct the prospect to a company website to do their research and learn more about the company (15 minutes)

* Network the prospect with an experienced company leader to get the prospect's questions answered (20 minutes)

Total time used: 40 minutes

Contrast that to a one-on-one meeting, which usually involves the following time commitment:

* Getting ready—shower, change, prepare (30 minutes)

* Driving time to/from meeting (30 minutes)

* Meeting time (60 minutes)

* Transition time to arrange next meeting (15 minutes)

Total time used: 135 minutes

Your success and financial future are directly related to the number of prospects you meet. With the organic approach, you can connect with at least four times as many potential prospects as you can when conducting one-on-one meetings. How is that for time management strategy!

Improve your life management skills by using all of the people, tools, and resources available. Each day, ask yourself which activities are the most important and pursue those tasks with absolute persistence. Be prepared for the unexpected, as well as to substitute a task from a list of other activities.

Remember, too, that each of us have talent in some areas and not in others. What matters is that you optimize your talents as you allocate the use of your time. Maybe you're not good at the accounting side of your business. Instead of wasting your time, rely on a neighbor or family member to assist you.

How you invest and manage the time of your life will contribute greatly to your desired outcomes. Gaining control of your time empowers you to take charge of your own destiny.

Chapter 15

THE IT FACTOR: BECOME A MASTER COMMUNICATOR

Have you ever wondered why some people start a conversation and immediately grab your attention, while others who may have something more valuable to say are often ignored? Are some people born with a special gift? Did they take a course on how to become charismatic? These questions have certainly crossed my mind over the years.

We've all seen people who possess the It Factor at social and business events. They enter a conference room and, within seconds, are engaged in a conversation with a total stranger! Meanwhile, you fidget in the corner, hoping that someone will recognize you and wander over to say, hello. Your hands get clammy; your brow sweats, and you wish the conference would start so that you can take a seat in relative obscurity. Once the conference begins, you discover the person who has been the center of attention is the guest speaker. Some people have all the luck, you think to yourself.

It's not luck. For organic networkers, it is about mastering the fundamental skills of communication, an essential part of Principle #8—Relationships. Communication enables you to create honest and powerful connections in meetings, social interactions, and relationships. While this may seem like an ambitious undertaking, becoming a master communicator is simply an organic process. You learn certain skills; you practice them, and you excel. This chapter is designed to assist you to acquire the It Factor in network marketing and in life.

The It Factor is also known as, charisma. Webster's Dictionary defines, charisma, as: A personal magic of leadership arousing special popular loyalty or enthusiasm for a public figure (such as a political leader); a special magnetic charm or appeal (such as a popular entertainer)

Nowhere in this definition does it say that a person is born with charisma, while another is eternally doomed to be a wallflower. Had that been the case, I would have given up years ago! Instead, I discovered two facts about the It Factor: I had to learn a specific set of communication skills, and I had to possess the willingness and burning desire to apply them in my life, which follows Principle #9—Wisdom.

To become a powerful, confident communicator requires energy and effort, but it gets easier with practice.

ORGANICWISE:

The It Factor is not something you are born with but can be developed organically over time. Start by learning the basic skills of good communication that build confidence. Practice these skills daily, and they will become second nature.

Walk with Confidence

Walking is one of the most basic human actions and doesn't require a lot of conscious effort. The way you walk communicates how others view you and is an expression of how confident you are in any given situation.

The Power Walk exudes confidence and requires your focus in three ways:

* Look Up: Hold your head up and maintain your glance at eye level. This creates opportunities to make eye contact. Think of it as a nonverbal way of saying, "Hi, how are you?"

* Swing Naturally: The swinging motion of your arms as you walk should be natural and not forced. If you restrict the natural motion, you will look stiff (or in need of the nearest bathroom). If you exaggerate the swing, you will probably look silly.

* Mind Your Things: Carry a purse or briefcase in such a way that you can walk comfortably. Lugging too much baggage will cause you to look stiff and lose that snap in your walk that transmits confidence.

Walking with confidence requires focus, practice, and discipline, as noted in Organic Principle #2—Discipline. Focus and practice until a confident walk becomes second nature, and get ready for numerous potential benefits, as walking tall is standing tall amid all of life's challenges.

Maintain Eye Contact

Ever wonder why it is difficult to look someone in the eye while engaged in a conversation? Psychologically, eye contact can be intimidating and uncomfortable. However, if you smile when you look someone in the eye, it connects you intimately with whomever you are talking with or to, whether it be a single individual, a small group, or a large audience. The magic of eye contact, when done properly, projects sincerity and openness and keeps the listener's attention focused on you.

Because of the intimacy factor of eye contact, shy people often struggle with it. If you tend to be nervous about looking someone in the eye who you are talking to, begin with a brief glance or look around their eye, or the end of their nose, instead of directly into their eyes. With practice, you will become more comfortable, and your shyness will diminish.

Cultural issues can also come into play. In North America, direct eye contact is as normal and expected as a firm handshake. This is not true, however, in other parts of the world. In Asia, Africa, and Latin America, people may avoid direct eye contact as a sign of respect. People from Middle Eastern countries, on the other hand, use prolonged eye contact to gauge trustworthiness. Different cultures within a single country may use eye contact differently. Pay attention to cultural differences, and if you are unsure about which eye contact is appropriate, check with someone who understands the customs of each region.

Dress for Success

One of the most overused phrases in business, dress for success, matters because first impressions are critical. You are not only marketing the products and opportunity of your company, you are marketing yourself to a potential colleague. Make every effort possible to dress appropriately. Will dressing well get you that new distributor? Not as a stand-alone proposition, but a positive first impression will give you a competitive edge. Like it or not, you will be judged by your appearance.

What is appropriate attire? My experience, as an organic networker, has been that dressing conservatively is always the safest route. This doesn't mean to go on a shopping spree and max your credit card. You can save shopping until you hit your first big financial goal. In the beginning of your career, it is important to have two or three sets of business attire to get you through every week.

When conducting business in a foreign country, be sure to know the cultural traditions for business attire. In Japan, for example, a white tie is not appropriate for meetings. In China, a red tie means, power, and displays your awareness of their culture. In some cultures, black ties are only worn at funerals.

SIDEBAR: CHECK YOUR LOOK

Your appearance for meetings should abide by this list:

- Clean, polished, and conservative dress shoes

- Well-groomed hair

- No body odor

- Strong cologne or perfume can be a turnoff to many people with allergies.

- Tattoos and body piercing are discouraged.

- Nothing is a bigger turnoff than halitosis.

- No gum or candy in your mouth

- Minimal jewelry

- Clean, trimmed fingernails

When You're Smiling

When it comes to the It Factor, a smile is like the welcome mat of your personality, making you instantly more approachable. Some people naturally have a terrific smile. Some of us have to work at it. One thing I can promise you, once you've mastered your smile, you'll consistently look better in pictures!

If smiling feels unnatural to you, you need to pay attention to what your smile-free face is communicating. You might enjoy your job but fail to show your pleasure. Maybe you want to meet someone, but your stoic face doesn't offer a friendly sign of your feelings. You can even be in love with somebody and totally hide it! If you want to connect with others, your face has to express the positive emotions you feel.

One way to become better at smiling is to observe other smiling folks around you. Notice how their smile makes them come across as warm and inviting. Think about a famous actor you recently watched in a movie. How did his or her smile affect how you saw the character in the film? One of my all-time favorite actresses is Goldie Hawn. Regardless of the role she plays, she has this radiant, alluring smile that is absolutely infectious.

Find your role models, then practice. Look in a mirror for a few moments and smile. Ask yourself if you look friendly and approachable. Do you like the image you're projecting? If you are feeling unsure, ask for some feedback from a close friend. Keep practicing until you find the smile that feels and looks right for you.

Stand Up for Yourself

Why do some people have excellent posture while others always slouch? To me, it has a lot to do with the physical challenges of a sedentary lifestyle. Lack of physical exercise and hours spent hunched in front of the computer screen wear down our bodies, contributing damage to our spine, rib cage, and joints.

Proper posture can literally change your life. You will feel better, experience less stress, and be better able to avoid the aches and pains associated with slouching. Your posture affects your level of confidence, which also affects posture. The more confident you are, the better your posture will be.

Here are some action steps to keep you standing or sitting tall:

Exercise Daily

Whether I am traveling or at home, I spend thirty to sixty minutes every day running, weight training, or doing some form of physical exercise. One of the reasons people can't find the time to work out is their lack of organizational skills, namely, time management. I've learned, over the years, to multitask in many areas of my life, including when I work out. I schedule most of my morning calls while I'm on a treadmill or elliptical. Therefore, I can manage two priorities at the same time. Today, I exercise five days a week without falling behind on my daily tasks and activities.

Keep It Moving

You're more likely to slouch if your job or daily activities involve a lot of sitting around. As your muscles tire from being in the same position, your body compensates by hunching over. You need to move! For those of you with office jobs, make it a habit to get up and move around for a couple of minutes, every half hour or so.

Keep Your Ears, Shoulders, and Hips in Alignment

Remember, organic networking is about building from the ground up. Your posture is like wearing an armored suit of confidence. People always want to do business with people who exude confidence in themselves. They want the confidence to rub off on them. The confidence you radiate will be on display whether you're standing or sitting. In either case, consciously improve your posture by keeping your ears, shoulders and hips in a straight vertical line. Always make certain that your ears are in line with your shoulders. Check your stance, and correct it when necessary.

Loosen Up

Using the straight vertical alignment while standing or sitting, you imitate a soldier at attention. Shift your body weight often, and keep your neck and knees flexible.

Avoid High Heels

To my female readers: If you don't need to wear higher heels, don't. High heels alter your body's center of gravity and throw your posture out of alignment. If heels are a must, consider dress shoes with lower heels.

Pick It Up

When you bend down to pick something up, don't bend at the waist, bend at the knees, keeping your spine straight.

These simple tips to improve your posture are easy to master, but even when people strive to consciously improve their posture, they can slouch for hours before remembering to correct themselves. That's the power of bad habits! I suggest that you keep a visual reminder to check your posture wherever you spend the most time. If you sit at a desk, sketch a human stick figure on a sticky note and attach it to your computer or phone. Every time you see it, ask yourself: How's my posture? Are my ears in line with my shoulders? Are my feet flat on the floor?

Stay Humble

Organic Principle #12—Humility doesn't come naturally to most of us, especially in today's busy and competitive world. We often see others take advantage of a situation to get ahead or to look good. Having the It Factor is not about looking good; it's about a goodness that people can see in you.

A humble person is grateful for the blessings he or she has received and is willing to share the good fortune. Being humble puts everything into perspective. Instead of thinking that you need to be the best at this or the finest at that, everyone is seen as equal on the most important and organic level. We each come with different strengths and weaknesses and, as an organic networker, it is important to bring out the best in others.

One of the ways I express this is through my interactions with audiences during the pre- and post-event functions at major events. I make it a point to connect with everyone possible during picture-taking times. I greet people with respect. I accommodate special requests and look for ways that I can encourage positive feelings. For example, when hugging people that are much short-er than me, I bend my knees so that I'm physically at their level. This makes people of smaller stature feel more comfortable and confident.

Here are other humbleness-building traits, taken from my own daily practice.

Thank Others

We never accomplish anything on our own. It always takes help from others, whether the assistance comes from your boss, fellow staffers, spouse, friends, or strangers. Behind every successful man or woman is a team. And this team usually gets very little recognition, despite how much they have done to contribute to the success of that person. Take every opportunity to thank others for what they do and how they help you.

When my mother and I settled in Greece, I couldn't be picky about the job I got, because I was very young and didn't yet speak any Greek. My first job was cleaning out big ships that docked in the harbor. I scrubbed and hosed down those wretchedly filthy ships seven days a week. In the evenings, I spent as much time as I could with boys in the neighborhood. My friendly nature made it easy for me to make friends, and my new friends taught me how to speak and understand Greek.

My mother and I were eventually able to rent a 300 square foot house with the money I earned. Each time I walked through the front door, I felt proud of myself for being able to be a good provider. I also longed for the day when I would never have to clean another smelly, disgusting ship.

When a busboy job opened up at a nearby restaurant, I jumped at the chance to make a change. My new job involved cleaning and setting tables, lugging dirty dishes into the kitchen, and helping the waiters. It was physical labor, but I always did my best. I also made it a point to thank my coworkers and treat them with respect. Several months later, a highly-coveted waiter position opened up. I really wanted that promotion, as waiters not only made a regular salary, they also earned extra money from tips. The restaurant owner recognized my hearty work ethic and how I treated people with respect. What sealed the deal in his mind were the accolades I got from my coworkers. I learned that many of my coworkers had approached the owner and urged him to give me the promotion.

While I knew it was important to treat people with kindness and respect, this experience inspired me to make treating people fairly a mission in life. A few years ago, I visited Greece and stopped by to see my old boss. He told me that some of the guys from my waiter days wanted to meet me for a drink. We're talking twenty-five years later! I was amazed and humbled that they would remember me.

Redirect Praise

I am a huge believer in redirecting praise, which I use as a way to stay humble, and I instill it in others. Playing down your own significance or self-importance, and sharing the fact that others had a role in your success, is especially important in work groups, as it drastically reduces the risk of anyone thinking you're someone who takes all the credit. If you deflect or redirect accolades, passing them along to the others involved and truly believe that you weren't that significant, it will go a long way toward developing a humble attitude.

You Don't Have to Be Right

A humble organic networker never tries to look better or smarter than others, including the habit of having to be right all of the time. Even when you respond to a statement with something like, I know, you are asserting dominance over another person. Instead of striving to prove that you are right, even if you know something already, simply say, "Interesting, thanks for that." Humble people are right about one thing; they are not always right!

Come in Second

When in a team or group environment, give others a chance to be the first to speak, share ideas, or get involved. This can be very humbling for several reasons. You might hear others present better or smarter ideas. Someone might even introduce something that you would have said if you'd had the chance to speak first!

It's not easy to accept that you're not the only one capable of a task or that you may not be as needed as you would like to imagine yourself to be. That's okay. That's reality! Be humble enough to see yourself as an important contributor who doesn't need to prove it by chiming in first.

Appreciate Everything

We often forget to be grateful for the little things because we get so focused on our busy lives and accomplishments. Appreciate your home and your loved ones. Give thanks for the health, wealth, and happiness you've experienced and the opportunities the future has to offer. Appreciation nurtures being humble. Look at nature. Think of the world and how awesome it is. Then, show this appreciation in your life.

Listen Up

By listening more than you speak, you gain insights into others. Being open to people is at the heart of Organic Principle #11—Respect. You practice being humble by listening intently and your response to what you have heard. Listening gives other people time to share their thoughts, feelings, and opinions. It also gives you time to absorb what they say.

Don't Judge Others

One very important aspect of being humble involves refusing to judge others. Judgment is a dangerous practice, closing you off from being open minded, empathetic, or appreciative of others. Everyone is different and comes with different ideas. When you judge, you are projecting that you have some special significance. To avoid this attitude, refer to Organic Principle #12—Humility.

Practice being humble by genuinely taking interest in what others have to say or do over time. Let their ideas play out without judgment. And, whatever you do, do not talk about people behind their backs.

SIDEBAR: CHECK YOUR EGO

Think about some of the ways you have judged other people in the past.

- ❖ What would you change about your past reactions?

- ❖ Did you think about what you said and how it may have affected them?

- ❖ Did you take more credit for something than you deserved?

- ❖ Did you want to prove you were right at the expense of someone else's feeling?

- ❖ Did you think that your contribution was more important than someone else's?

- ❖ Did you arrogantly let people know that you were smarter than them?

- ❖ Did you brag about things you did or can do?

How would you want to be treated, if you were on the receiving end of your own thoughts and actions? Answer that question, and you'll learn to check your ego at the door!

Speak and Be Heard

I was fortunate to listen to someone I consider one of the best speakers in our profession. After watching and listening to his presentation, I realized he was the public speaking role model I wanted to emulate. True to Principle #9—Wisdom, I became a sponge and began to study him. One thing I took note of was his speaking technique. He could capture people's attention within thirty seconds. In addition to his tone of voice, his gestures and eye contact seemed to contribute to his connection with his audiences.

I also noticed how tough it was for the next person to walk on stage and follow his presentation. In comparison to my mentor's powerful speaking style, most speakers were painfully weak in their delivery. Hearing the difference in presentation skills inspired me to practice speaking for hours in front of a mirror every week. Whether my audience was one person or a thousand, I knew that the delivery of my speech was as important as what I had to say.

Develop Your Voice

A high, whiny voice is never perceived as one of authority. In fact, it can make you sound like prey to an aggressive prospect or colleague who is out to make his or her point at the expense of someone else. Deepen your voice by doing exercises to lower the pitch. You can always hire a voice coach, or here is a fun exercise I used: Sing your favorite songs an octave lower than you normally sing. Over a period of time, you will find it easier to speak in a deeper voice.

Slow Down

Talking too fast will make people nervous and uninterested in anything you have to say. On the other hand, don't overcompensate and slow your speech to a point that you put people to sleep. Be careful not to slow down to the point where people begin to finish your sentences.

I sometimes get caught up in a fast-paced conversation that goes on for a long period of time, and suddenly, I realize that I lost my audiences at, hello. I usually gauge my speaking style by looking directly at people and checking their attention level and participation to see if they are tracking the content of my conversation.

A good way to pace a conversation is to pause, ask a question, and reply. Pause as often as you can, and keep your sentences short.

I always keep in mind these words of wisdom from Shakespeare, *"Men of few words are the best men."*

Animate Your Voice

Avoid speaking in a monotone. Your pitch should always shift higher or lower with the major points of your message. If you need an example of good vocal animation, listen to your local TV news anchor and take notes.

Enunciate Your Words

Speak clearly, enunciating your words. We've all known people who mumble, whose words are often impossible to understand. If people are always saying, huh, to you when you speak, you are probably mumbling.

Watch the Volume

The rule of thumb is to choose a volume that is appropriate for the setting. Speak more softly when you are in a small, personal setting. When you are speaking to larger groups or across large spaces, it's proper to speak louder.

Pronounce Words Correctly

People will judge your competency through your vocabulary. If you aren't sure how to pronounce a word, it's best to not use it until you understand proper usage.

Use the Right Words

If you're not sure of the meaning of a word, don't use it. However, I recommend that you practice learning and using a new word every day.

Get in Touch

Your words, vocal qualities, and message must match. The same rules apply to your gestures and facial expressions. When it comes to using body language to get your messages across, I advise that you use smaller facial expressions and gestures for individuals and small groups. Save the big, sweeping gestures as the group you are addressing increases in size.

Body Language

Body language also includes physical touch. Used carefully and appropriately, touching can be a very effective way to enhance your communications skills. I see, touch, as falling into four categories:

* Social touch – is ideal if you want to be seen as a cordial person and is a common occurrence at parties and social gatherings. Friends and close business associates may hug, kiss, or do a two-handed handshake as a way of saying that it's great to see you.

* Friendly touch – is as simple as a pat on the back or on a shoulder. It's a small gesture, but it may mean a lot to someone who needs comfort and support and is a great way to give praise, as well.

* Intimate touch – is only shared by individuals who have developed a deep bond with each other. As the name suggests, this is usually reserved for the loving affection between couples.

* Professional touch – is what you receive from your therapist, physician, dentist, or hairdresser, offering reassurance and comfort.

Mind Your Message

Effective communication must be clear of any ambiguity that will confuse the recipient and may lead to missed opportunities. When I have an important presentation or meeting, I rely on Organic Principle #1—Readiness and plan in advance the clear and distinct message I want to get across to my audience. My planning step involves writing down the key points I want to convey to my intended audience. I write short sentences in bullet point form, outlining the key phrases and questions I plan to review. Then, I rehearse in front of a mirror, taking stock of how I want to communicate my presentation. Communication is critically important in organic networking. Winging it is never a good idea.

Practice and Get It

I practice what I preach every day. By practicing what you've learned in this chapter, I am confident you will become a master communicator, someone with the It Factor, the hallmark of a successful organic network.

We have a basic choice in business and in life: We either take control or we let others take control away from us.

Chapter 16

ORGANIC INVESTING FOR MAXIMUM ROI

Unlike traditional businesses, where your success typically requires a significant financial investment, organic networking is a unique business system in which your investment is based upon the following equation:

Time + Effort = Success

You build your business from the ground up with the vision of achieving long-term results without cutting corners. The idea of spending months, or even years, before seeing a positive Return On Investment (ROI) is hard for some people to accept. I was not one of those people!

Let's say that you invest 15 hours a week in your business and your time is worth $20 per hour. That means you are investing about $300 per week or $1,200 per month. During the early months, you will generate less ROI (dollars earned) as compared to your initial start-up investment (time invested). However, as you grow your business over the coming months, there's potential for moving into positive cash flow.

In 2001, when I started building my second network marketing business, I was working 50 to 60 hours a week and earning less than $250 per week. My $250 per week divided by 50 hours came to about $5 per hour! That is less than minimum wage in most Western countries. However, as time progressed and my business began to grow, my earnings increased to over $2,500 per week. With the same 50-hour week, I was making about $50 per hour for doing the same amount of work. Two years later, holding fast to Principle #6— Persistence, I increased my income to $25,000 per week. I had also reduced my weekly time investment to about 25 hours per week, or half the time I had originally invested each week, to yield these results.

Over the course of a few short years, my ROI went from $5 per hour to about $1,000 per hour. And, based on my experience, it took far less time to achieve a return in organic networking than in a conventional business. Without an understanding of how ROI works in this profession, would I have agreed to work for less than minimum wage during those early months? Probably not, but there's nothing like the promise of earning substantial income to reinforce how well the ROI system can work.

SIDEBAR: YOUR ROI

In this profession, your true ROI is what you believe you are worth. If you believe you're worth $50 per hour, then perhaps you won't need to wait a few years to see your ROI. It comes down to your expectations. Since the majority of people in organic network marketing work part-time, if your expectation level is set correctly, you understand the long-term process, and you know what true ROI means, there's a good chance that you will achieve your target ROI.

Saving and Investing

When my ROI hit about $25,000 per week, I was earning a lot of money but saving very little. One day, I had a serious talk with my mentor about saving money that awakened me from any financial drowsiness. While there are countless articles on how to save and invest your money, I am going to tell you about the organic savings system that worked for me and for many of my millionaire colleagues in network marketing. I call this process the Invest and Build System.

No matter how much money you're earning in your business, you must set aside an amount for investment retirement purposes. Open a long-term savings account that is for untouchable funds. Treat this money as if it were no longer available to you. Even if you can initially set aside only a few dollars out of every paycheck, do it. Even $10 per week will add up to an additional $520 per year in savings.

> ## ORGANICWISE:
>
> Organic investing starts with the first earning and carries over to your investment portfolio. For most organic networkers, a portfolio is built one dollar at a time. That's why it is crucial to understand the organic strategies shared in this chapter to ensure your ROI.

The Invest and Build System

Once you've reached an income level of **$1,000 per week or more** in your business, start following this investment process to the letter:

* ❖ Transfer 10 percent of your weekly or monthly income immediately into your long-term savings account.

- ❖ Apply 40 percent of your weekly or monthly income toward paying your personal bills and household expenses. Be smart and spend it wisely.

- ❖ The remaining 50 percent of your weekly or monthly income must be invested back into your business.

Once you've reached an income level of **$5,000 per week or more**, you should follow these guidelines:

- ❖ Transfer 20 percent of your weekly or monthly income immediately into your long-term savings account.

- ❖ Put 30 percent of your weekly or monthly income towards paying your personal bills and household expenses. Again, spend this money wisely.

- ❖ 50 percent of your weekly or monthly income goes back into your business.

When you've reached earnings of **$10,000 per week or more**, you adhere to this investment plan:

- ❖ 30 percent of your weekly or monthly income gets immediately transferred to your long-term savings account.

- ❖ 30 percent of your weekly or monthly income goes towards paying your personal bills and household expenses.

- ❖ 40 percent of your weekly or monthly income goes back into your business.

Trust me, this entire process is a lot easier than it sounds. After starting the Invest and Build System for myself, I soon realized that it was much easier to have my savings automatically deducted from my checks. Most banks and investment firms offer such a service. Having funds electronically transferred into your not-to-be-touched savings account also protects you from the temptation of spending any extra money. Principle #2—Discipline also applies to financial discipline. It is your adherence to financial discipline that will make the difference in the long run.

A couple of years ago, one of my close friends and team members approached me on the subject of organic investing. She had recently gone through some financial hardship but was now experiencing her first year of measurable ROI. In just thirty minutes on the phone, I was able to put together a plan for her that mapped out how she would build her investment portfolio over the next two years.

At the time, she was earning about $2,500 per week. I advised her to have 20 percent of each weekly check automatically transferred to a stand-alone savings account. These funds, I told her, are money you should not think of as yours, at least in the short term. It was hard for her to digest this, initially. However, eighteen months later we both attended an event in Dallas. My friend asked me to join her for lunch, as she was excited to share some news with me.

Over lunch, she said, "Thanks to you, Kosta, I have been able to put aside $37,000 by following the advice you gave me over a year ago." She told me that while she had once had a job that paid her a high six-figure income, she was never able to save liquid cash like this in such a short period of time. I responded, "My dear, the only thing I ask you to do for me is to pay it forward. Share your wisdom with your future team members and friends."

SIDEBAR: CHARITIES AND INCOME TAXES

Please remember to set funds aside for your favorite charities and your income taxes according to your country's tax laws. A great investment in itself is consulting with a knowledgeable accountant who has a full understanding of home-based businesses (check out SOHO.org) and the limitations to writing off charities and business expenses versus personal expenses.

Dealing with Debts

There is considerable debate on the merits of investing versus paying off your debts. The reality is that personal debt is a huge problem all over the world. Debt, be it from credit cards, student loans, bank loans, personal lines of credit, or car loans, brings with it financial commitments that could rob a person of his or her future income. That may sound severe, but think about it. In order to own something, now, people commit to loan or credit card repayment in the future. College students borrow thousands of dollars each year to pay tuition, but there's no guarantee of finding a job after graduation. Many unemployed people are using credit cards just to get by.

The first step in any debt reduction plan is to stop accruing debt. In the case of credit card debt, the first step is to stop charging on those cards, immediately. To paraphrase a comment I heard recently, "Failure is a simple error in judgment repeated over time, you can't pay down debt if you are still adding to it!" Examine your income and decide how much money you need monthly for living expenses, food, gas, and utilities. Then, choose a monthly dollar amount to apply toward your debt and stick to it.

Your second step is to look at the interest rate you are paying on your credit cards. Most people owe on more than one card. Pay off the debt on your highest interest-bearing credit card first. This will save you money in the long run, even if that card is not the one with the biggest balance. Store charge cards usually have exorbitant interest rates that the merchant will not reduce. Luckily, these are the credit cards you need the least. The average person should have one to two major credit cards in order to maintain a decent credit score and in case of unforeseeable emergencies.

If you are in college with student loans, you may not be able to focus on reducing debt until you graduate and find steady work.

Once you graduate, the loan agency will put you on a repayment schedule, usually based on your income. If you have multiple lenders, it may be beneficial to consolidate loans with one lender. Unconsolidated loans are often subject to interest rate fluctuations with increasing rates.

When considering loan consolidation, consult with a loan advisor to determine the best course of action for you. If you find that you can't consolidate, always pay off the private student loans before chipping away at the lower-interest government loans. Private student loans have high interest rates and cannot be deferred if you fall on hard times and can't make the payments.

Since debt is a part of most people's lives today, any steps you take now to reduce debt will motivate you to save a lump sum at the end of the year. Seeing your savings grow will fire you up far more than seeing your debt slowly decrease.

Investing in Your Business

This section is by far the most important one in this chapter. That's because every dollar you put back into your business can be considered either an investment or a business expense. Invest your ROI-boosting dollars in one or more of these actions:

- ❖ **Attend events.** Attending company or team events, conventions, and boot camps is a top priority in your business. Make sure to include your team and family members.

- ❖ **Purchase training programs.** Principle #9—Wisdom states that you ensure the possibility of long-term success by educating yourself and your leadership team. Invest in appropriate, relevant, third-party training programs.

- ❖ **Buy the right tools.** Just as a carpenter needs woodworking tools to build a table, an organic networker needs the right tools to build a business properly and efficiently.

Examples include: computers, smart phones, projectors, flip chart easels, and team management systems.

❖ **Update your image.** Selecting and purchasing the most appropriate attire will potentially influence how clients and prospects perceive you.

❖ **Go the distance.** To advance your business to the next level, it may be necessary to travel to other cities or other countries to build your business. For me, this is one of the top three areas to consider when investing back into your business.

❖ **Take care of your team.** Investing in your team is one of the best ways to create excitement and momentum. This ties in to Principle #8—Relationships. If managed correctly, team-building activities can anchor your business.

Investment Wise

Here are some final rules for investing your money:

❖ **Don't let a small loss become BIG.** Don't keep losing money just to prove you are right. At the same time, refuse to waste time supporting people who are not producing results. When all you are left with is hope, get out and look for a new leader.

❖ **If you don't understand the strategy of the company or group, don't invest in it.** It's not unusual for your company to introduce new strategies for growing or expanding the business. As a potential investor, refuse to be wooed. Either make an effort to understand the strategy or say, no thanks. Experience has shown me that it's better not to stray too far from what I know. When presented with an opportunity, I do my research first. If I'm not satisfied with my findings, I don't invest until I have a complete grasp of the plan.

South Korea was one of my stops when I travelled throughout Asia a few years back. While I was there, I met with a number of individuals and groups that had shown interest in my company. At first, I was extremely moved with their presentation and vision. My past experiences, however, made me cautious. Pushing doubts aside, I decided to dive into the process and try to understand what the group was bringing to the table. Two days later, after hours of meeting late into the night, I finally concluded that it was not the right business investment for me. My decision pivoted on one issue: their strategy. No matter how hard I studied the proposal, I couldn't wrap my mind around it completely.

Expressing my thanks, I moved on. As I continued on my travels throughout Asia, I kept in touch with them. A few months later, news came through the grapevine that the South Korean group had joined another company and had been financially rewarded. Unfortunately, they ended up falling short in delivering on what they had promised. Soon after, they were on the scavenger hunt again. I was lucky! If I had invested in that group, it could have been an extremely costly experience for me. That's why I recommend that you fully understand a company or group strategy before you invest.

❖ **Maintain ongoing incentives for your team.** As a leader, you will run promotions to motivate your team. Over the years, I've given away dozens of major prizes, including vacation trips, jewelry, watches, designer wear, cash, and even a brand new Porsche convertible, not to mention the thousands of other smaller incentives I put in place to fuel my team's burning desire. If done right, you should be able to have a 10-to-1 ROI, long term. Believe it or not, promotions also contribute to long-term loyalty and happiness within your team.

Run promotions long term to let them get firmly established, and make sure they are timely and current. If a promotion runs too long, however, it will be forgotten.

❖ **Travel and entertainment investments are extremely rewarding, if done right.** The hundreds of travel or wine-and-dine investments I've made to support or reward individuals with real potential have paid off. I watched as many of those folks went on to become top income earners. That is the beauty of organic network marketing. You only need about 30 percent of your investment dollars to build a highly successful team. Contrast that to a traditional business, where you need 75 percent of your investments to pay off and get a reasonable return.

Always set goals and parameters on when and how you will spend this money. The people you want to acknowledge and reward are the team members who are producing results. Your expenses need to be in line with the type of ROI you want to achieve.

❖ **Invest in You.** In closing this chapter, I want to leave you with this: We all want to invest wisely and to achieve a high level of success. Remember to move forward with your heart, instead of just listening to your head. This inner voice is often the one that directs us toward the most satisfying outcome.

Chapter 17

THE ART OF NEGOTIATION

I attribute my attitude on organic negotiation to my upbringing in the Persian culture and conducting business in multiple countries and societies. On some level, I have become hardwired that everything is open to negotiation. I am surprised that in many Western countries, negotiating is considered taboo. I have yet to witness a customer walk into Nordstrom, Wal-Mart, or other stores and automatically negotiate the full sticker price or marked down price on products or services.

In my experience, I have found that building a network marketing business is no different from building a business that takes a huge down payment, net worth, inventory, building, and so on, before you can open the doors. You must make every penny count. Therefore, I believe that we have a basic choice in business and in life: We either take control, or we let others take control. That makes negotiation and making deals a vital part of our day-to-day life.

Make Negotiating a Part of Everyday Life

At home, you may make deals with your children to change behavior, such as clean their room, study, improve their grades, or swear off drugs and alcohol. In marriages and partnerships, spouses or significant others negotiate regularly over many of life's simple, day-to-day issues.

Negotiation obviously takes two people, and many times you will negotiate with groups of people. For instance, you can negotiate dates to meet goals, such as the number of activities, like prospecting calls to be made per day or week. When two or more people are involved in negotiating, there can be some tension or conflict.

As I mentioned, negotiating has become a way of life for me. Negotiating in the Eastern culture is much different than in the Western culture. As a matter of fact, even in these cultures where negotiating is a way of life, the rules may vary. For instance, in some cultures, it is acceptable to look in the eye at whomever you are negotiating with; in other cultures, it is taboo.

I am much better, today, at interacting and negotiating with people on all levels of my life. I've learned from the best and encourage you to do the same. To me, one of the very best is Roger Dawson, a world-renowned negotiation expert. Attending his lectures, reading his books, and listening to his audio recordings has helped me master the art of negotiation, in whichever culture I am conducting business, using my personal style. Some of the most effective techniques I have learned from Dawson are in this chapter. I've refined these methods through trial and error, over many years. Before we get into rules of organic negotiations, let's look at some skills for *reading* the people with whom you are negotiating.

* **Find Your Leverage.** When negotiating with teams or individuals, you must figure out clues that will give you

an advantage. Whether you are a manager, team leader, facilitator, or negotiator on the other side of the table, watch for clues.

* **Verbal Clues.** If the group or person whom you are negotiating with changes the tenor of their voice—if their pitch goes up—they are probably trying to disagree. This is an advantage to you, since you can analyze the disagreement, make course corrections, and move the negotiations in the direction of acceptance and agreement. This could translate into big success for you in that particular component of the negotiations.

* **Eye Contact.** Is the person or group you are negotiating with engaged by looking you in the eye, or are they looking away or practicing other types of eye contact avoidance? Clues like these help you to identify the level of agreement or disagreement in the room. I always pay close attention to people's eye contact during negotiation. Whenever faced with a gaze that feels angry, or if I notice that a person's eyes look down or away, in a way that feels defensive, I pull back to ask questions. This brings everyone back to square one and puts whomever I am negotiating with at ease. This also enables uncertain or defensive listeners to raise their heads and look at me when they answer my questions.

* **A Smile Is Worth Everything.** I've been involved in many serious conversations where the other party participated with a smiling and happy face. Their attitude made me relax and engage in every word they spoke. I also saw that these people were more open to the give-and-take in negotiating. People who negotiate with a frown on their face will seldom find a receptive audience.

* **Your Body Says It All.** In my early days, I could never figure out why some people crossed their arms and came across as close-minded whenever I was negotiating with an individual or a group. Then my mentor shared a

secret on how to help avoid this uncomfortable situation, and I found that his advice was one of my motivators for developing Organic Principle #5—Initiative.

When negotiating, you want to create an atmosphere that encourages open mindedness and eliminates defensive or close-minded behavior. Before you start negotiating, get everyone in the group talking about their favorite topic, themselves. As they talk, you must listen intently and be genuinely interested and soak up their information. When it comes time to negotiate, they will stay open minded and actively participate in the meeting. Although no two people are the same, most of us tend to react more positively if we feel that whomever we are talking to cares about us.

Never Break the Rules

The art of negotiation has its own set of rules. To win at the negotiating table, or to walk away without losing your shirt when there is no win, follow these rules faithfully:

❖ **The Law of Predictability.** First, learn to ask the right questions. Case in point: An experienced attorney will always ask a witness questions to which he already knows the answer. The legal profession refers to this as, the Law of Predictability. The attorney is following certain rules, which are associated with the process of questioning someone on the witness stand in order to get to the information he wants.

What I have learned about the art of negotiation is that many successful people in business tell us to start with the end result in mind. Today, I go into every negotiation with this mindset. Before I learned the rules of negotiating, I didn't have a desired outcome in mind, which many times brought disastrous results. I ended up losing more than I was prepared to lose. The organic negotiator always has a crystal clear vision of exactly what he wants to accomplish, so that he can remain focused and unwavering.

❖ **Know When to Walk Away.** As the old Kenny Rogers song goes: You gotta know when to hold 'em, know when to fold 'em. For example, whenever you walk into a car dealership to purchase an automobile or a furniture store to purchase furniture or any store to purchase products, you need to be prepared to walk out without purchasing a single product. If you get emotionally attached to the outcome, the deal, you might find yourself caving in to the salesperson's bargaining techniques and writing a check for the full amount because you did not follow the rules of negotiation and couldn't bring yourself to make a clean exit.

Knowing when to fold 'em has helped me tremendously in my real estate endeavors. Over the last decade, I have learned to restrain my passion for a certain property. This puts me in a position where I can negotiate better and maintain the upper hand. This practice has also saved me a fortune.

❖ **Don't reveal your deadline and limit(s).** When you show your cards too early, you give away the farm. The message you transmit is how desperately you need to make something happen, and that gives the power to the other person.

A few years ago, determined to purchase a new car, I was at a car dealership. Although I needed the car immediately, I never divulged my intent, which could give the salesman a distinct advantage. Since the transaction would take place in the last third of the month, a time slot when salespeople are driven to meet their numbers, I knew that I had the advantage in negotiating a bigger discount.

The salesman soon realized that he needed to reduce the cost in order to make his quota, but he held his own, and I walked out of the dealership. He was probably frantic. The very next day, he called me, and not only did he offer me a significant discount, he also threw in $500 worth of free, branded apparel if I purchased that day. At that point, I accepted his offer. We both won, and I got everything I wanted.

❖ **Use Organic Principal #11—Respect.** Fortunately, I have conducted business in multiple cultures and have travelled the globe three times. Because of my travels, I have a tremendous grasp on what it takes to be an effective negotiator in different cultures where this knowledge is critical.

The first time I had an opportunity to experience negotiations in a different culture was in the late '90s, when I travelled to Asia to negotiate with local leadership. Unlike in North America, where we negotiate first, celebrate our victory, and then get to know the people from the other side of the table, the negotiation process in Asian countries begins with relationship building. I learned this the hard way with the local Asian leadership over the first two days. The whole process took patience and the ability to stay engaged.

I learned that you must be able to adapt to local traditions very quickly. In addition, if you don't build a relationship first, it will be a reality check. The door will close to any successful negotiation. Proper negotiation has to do with your character, which will be the trust builder before a single dollar is negotiated. Understanding your opponent's culture will pay off tenfold in the long run.

❖ **Use Organic Principal #7—Patience.** If you are prepared, ready, and patient, Organic Principle #7—Patience will give you confidence and you will get the most out of your negotiation. Why? Because you'll be able to display a relaxed composure, and the other party will usually cave in and adapt to your end of the negotiation. I took this advice to heart and remained patient, cool, calm, and collected, when I was building my business in Korea. This attitude enabled me to be more flexible and powerful during negotiations, over the course of about eighteen months. That was difficult to endure! I wanted to give up many times, for many reasons. However, as part of my strategy, I implemented Organic Principle #6—Persistence, and this deal ended up being one of the most profitable ventures of my professional career. Had I been impatient and thrown in the towel, I would have lost close to a quarter of a million dollars in profit. The next time you think that a negotiation is taking too long, remember this story and imagine the potential loss if you let impatience win.

❖ **Keep Your Options Open.** I am a huge believer in being prepared with multiple options, in business and in life. Organic Principle #1—Readiness instructs us to have a Plan B whenever possible. Daily life doesn't always go as planned, and negotiations are no different. If the other party knows you are considering additional options, they tend to be more flexible. They may even bend some rules in order to accommodate you and avoid the potential loss of your business. In many cases, having multiple options can wear down your opponent.

During some negotiations about a decade ago, the other party and I came to a stalemate after two days of going back and forth with little progress. A few weeks later, I shared the stalemate with one of my mentors. He opened my eyes to how to use options that would have saved me the grief and hundreds of thousands of dollars. From that day on, I learned to always have more than one option at my disposal.

To summarize the Organic Rules of Negotiation:

- Have a clear end in mind.

- Don't be emotionally attached or desperate.

- Know when to hold 'em.

- Know when to fold 'em.

- Learn your opponent's culture.

- Be patient and stay in it for the long haul.

- Understand how valuable the right-minded negotiation process is to you, personally and financially.

ORGANICWISE:

An organic negotiator knows how important it is to understand the rules of negotiating. The goal is a win-win. Build the relationship first, and then plant the seeds for financial prosperity in the long run.

Make It a Win-Win

In organic networking, we constantly negotiate with team members, upline, suppliers, and the company, and it is often about money. If negotiations are conducted correctly and with the right intentions, you will create a win-win outcome in almost every instance. Negotiations should always be conducted with the best of intentions, especially when it comes to loved ones and people close to you. Always remember, in network marketing you are negotiating for success and to put profit in your team's and your bank account.

I understand that not many people take to negotiating as I do. On the other hand, it is important to understand that if you practice what I've shared in this chapter, no one will ever take control away from you at the negotiating table. You will learn to incorporate the art of negotiation in building your organization, and it will make and save you money.

GROWING FORWARD

Continuous action fuels motivation. Persist in your vision until you know that nothing will stop you from reaching your goals.

Plant Today – Harvest for Life

Organic Networker is your blueprint for building success in network marketing. I encourage you to read this book several times until the concepts and principles are etched into your brain.

Success in network marketing can be encapsulated in the following equation:

12 Organic Principles for Success + Organic Networking = Lifetime Residuals